Knowing God More

Knowing
God More

**A JOURNEY FROM BELIEF TO
GREATER INTIMACY**

Kevin M. Jackson, PhD

ISBN-13: 9798280547148

Dedication

To my beloved wife, Dr. Nila Nash-Jackson—Your love, prayers, and unwavering support have been the steady hand that has strengthened me through every season. You are my daily reminder of God's faithfulness, and I am forever grateful for the joy, wisdom, and partnership you bring into my life. Thank you for believing in the calling God placed upon me and for standing beside me as I pursue it with all my heart.

And to my mentor, Bishop Dr. Cheryl McBride Brown—Your example of steadfast faith, wisdom, and spiritual leadership has been a guiding light in my journey. Your encouragement and prophetic insight served as a spark of inspiration for this work. I honor you for all you have poured into my life and for the countless ways you have modeled what it means to walk closely with God.

This book is a tribute to the seeds you both have sown—seeds that have taken root and now bear fruit for the glory of God.

With deepest love and gratitude,

Dr. Kevin M. Jackson

Table of Contents

Acknowledgments

I am profoundly grateful to the mentors who have poured into my life and helped shape my journey in preaching, teaching, and ministry—Dr. Derrick Reaves, Dr. Barbara Amos, Dr. Norris Darden, and Dr. Stephanie Johnson. Your wisdom, example, and unwavering encouragement have deeply influenced the servant-leader I am today. Thank you for challenging me to pursue excellence, always for the glory of God.

To my children—Ephraim (Trinity), Elim, and Elisha—you are my greatest earthly joy and legacy. Watching you grow has been one of the most profound ways God continues to teach me about His love, patience, and purpose.

To my host of spiritual sons and daughters—LaMarr (Stephanie), Marquis, Quayshanna (Dev), LaToya, Starra, Jason (Marla), Brandon (Tiphany), Devon, Carlton, Dominic, Jared, Charles, Jordan (ShaRay), and Jonathan (Kelli), Jonathan (Heather), and Kenneth, and Garrett-Thank you for your prayers, your encouragement, and your trust. You have reminded me again and again why this work matters: to build lives anchored in Christ and committed to His Kingdom.

To all who have prayed, believed, and journeyed with me—this book is as much a reflection of your investment as it is my offering.

To God be the glory!!

The Invitation to More

Have you ever wondered if there's more to being saved than what you're experiencing right now? Maybe your relationship with God has settled into a routine, and you've grown comfortable—perhaps even complacent. Yet deep down, you sense there *has* to be more—more joy, more intimacy, more power in your walk with Him. If that resonates with you, consider this your divine invitation to recalibrate, rediscover, and renew what you once knew about God. He is always speaking, always revealing, and always drawing us closer—not just for today, but for every season of our lives.

Just like any meaningful relationship—whether in marriage, friendship, or between a parent and child—growth and deeper connection require intentionality. Relationships evolve over time, shaped by new seasons that bring fresh understanding, unexpected challenges, and opportunities for deeper love. The same is true in our walk with Christ. A thriving relationship with Jesus doesn't just happen—it must be nurtured, pursued, and continually refreshed.

This journey is about moving beyond where you are now and stepping into a deeper, more intimate relationship with God—one where knowing Him isn't just an intellectual belief but a daily life-transforming experience.

This book is designed to lead you on a path of discovery—one that carries present, future, and eternal significance. As you grow in your knowledge of God, you will inevitably embark on a journey of self-discovery as well. Your identity, purpose, and destiny are intertwined with knowing Him more deeply.

With each chapter, you will find moments of transformation—not just through reading but through engaging in thought-provoking discussions, meditating on key scriptures, and accessing additional resources designed to spark renewal, restoration, and revival in your heart and spirit.

This is more than just a book—it's an open invitation to encounter God in a fresh and life-changing way. He is calling you to deeper waters, to places of greater trust, joy, and revelation. Are you ready to go deeper?

If your answer is YES!, then I invite you to join me in this prayer of commitment—a sacred agreement between you and God as you embark on this journey:

Father, open my eyes so that I may see You more clearly. Open my ears so that I may hear Your voice with greater clarity. Awaken my heart, refresh my spirit, and stir my soul with a renewed passion for You. Remove any distractions or barriers that hinder my pursuit of You. As I walk through these pages, let me not only discover more about myself but, most importantly, more about You. Let this be the beginning of a lifelong pursuit of knowing You more.

In Jesus' Mighty Name, Amen.

Are you ready? Let's begin.

CHAPTER 1
Knowing God for Real

Discovering the Creator, Christ, and Our Faith

For many of us, our first introduction to God came through Sunday School lessons, Bible Study sessions, and other religious gatherings. These formative experiences laid a foundation, providing us with an understanding of who God is and who Christ is according to Scripture. Yet, there is a vast difference between knowing about God and truly knowing Him.

It is imperative that our foundational understanding of God is rooted in truth—truth that is firmly established in the biblical text. If we do not know the God of the Bible and His Son, Jesus Christ, how can we claim to be in right relationship with Him? The Word of God is His written revelation, unveiling who He is and how He has revealed Himself to humanity throughout history. From Genesis to Revelation, we are given insight into the nature, character, and works of God, as well as the redemptive mission of Jesus Christ.

God as Creator

One of the most fundamental truths we come to understand about God is that He is the Creator. The opening chapters of Genesis paint a picture of a God who spoke the universe into existence. "Let there be..." and with those words, everything became as He intended (Genesis 1:3). This foundational truth sets the stage for our understanding of His power, authority, and sovereignty over all creation.

God's Nature Revealed in the New Testament

The New Testament further deepens our understanding of God's nature. In the Gospel of John, we are reminded that: "God is spirit, and those who worship Him must worship in spirit and truth" - (John 4:24).

This crucial distinction helps us grasp that God is not a human being—He is spirit, transcendent, and omnipotent. At the same time, we recognize the mystery of Christ's incarnation: God wrapped in human flesh, dwelling among us to lead humanity to redemption through His sacrificial death and victorious resurrection on the third day (John 1:14).

These fundamental beliefs shape our perception of who God is and how Christ relates to the Father. They also establish the necessary foundation for our faith. The book of Hebrews reminds us: "Without faith, it is impossible to please God" - (Hebrews 11:6).

Faith is not merely an abstract concept; it is: "The substance of things hoped for and the evidence of things not seen" - (Hebrews 11:1).

Believing in God—who He is, what He has done, and what He can do—is the bedrock of our spiritual journey.

Without this foundation, we become vulnerable to false doctrines and the deceptions of man. It is only through a deep, unwavering understanding of the true God of the Bible that we can stand firm in our faith and pursue an authentic relationship with Him.

Meeting God Through His Son

It is crucial to understand that a true relationship with God can only be established through His Son, Jesus Christ. This relationship begins with the recognition that we are sinners in need of a Savior. It involves believing that Christ died on the cross for our sins and trusting in Him with the same certainty as we know our own name. In doing so, we step into salvation. Through this confession, we enter a new life of discipleship, growing ever more into the likeness of Christ.

A Call to Salvation

Brothers and sisters, if you have not yet made that decision, let us take a moment now to make your election sure. Simply repeat this prayer from your heart:

Father, I acknowledge that I am a sinner, and I desperately want to be in relationship with You through Your Son, Jesus Christ. Forgive me of my sins and cast them away as far as the east is from the west. God, I may not know everything about Jesus, but I do know that He died for my sins, that He is Your Son, and that He rose from the dead on the third day. Today, I welcome Christ into my heart with full understanding that I now belong to You. Thank You for this day of salvation. In Jesus' Name, Amen.

If you prayed that prayer with sincerity, you have entered into the family of God! Or perhaps you have renewed your commitment to salvation because you felt led by the Holy Spirit to recommit to a more vibrant relationship with Christ. Whatever your decision, thank God for it! You will never regret this choice—it is one that will follow you all the way into eternity.

Why Does Theology Matter?

Now, we move forward in our journey to understand what all of this knowledge about God truly means. In essence, this understanding shapes our theology—how we think about God, His existence, and His role in our lives. Theology is not just an abstract concept for scholars; it is a fundamental part of every believer's faith. It shapes how we live, how we worship, and how we perceive the world around us.

Imagine a man setting out on a road trip, relying on a faulty GPS that keeps leading him in the wrong direction. Later, he realizes he never updated the maps. In the same way, if our understanding of God is based on misinformation, outdated traditions, or cultural distortions, we may be heading in the wrong spiritual direction. This analogy highlights the dangers of distorted information and how it can impact an individual's path in life.

Your theology is best shaped by being an active part of a faith community—a local church—where you receive ongoing teaching about who God is and what those truths mean in practical terms. This is an essential part of Christian discipleship. Yes, individuals can read books—even books like this one—but as I have stated before, the foundation of truth for believers must always be the Word of the Lord. Any study of God, spirituality, and Christian discipleship must be firmly rooted in biblical text. Because it influences every aspect of your life.

Take a moment to consider these areas of your life:

Family Life – Your theological perspective will shape how you raise your children, how you view marriage, and how you relate to your family members.

Stewardship – Your understanding of God's principles will guide your financial decisions, how you handle money, and your ethical transactions.

Social Issues – Your theology will impact your stance on environmental issues, social justice, equality, and other societal matters.

Entertainment Choices – Your theological convictions will influence the kind of entertainment you consume and the activities you participate in as a believer.

Relationships with Others – Your theology shapes how you treat strangers, immigrants, fellow believers, and even those who oppose biblical values.

Political Views – Yes, even your political decisions and affiliations are impacted by your theological framework.

As you can see, understanding who God truly is and ensuring that your theology aligns with biblical truth is of utmost importance. If our beliefs about God are incorrect or misinformed, we risk living in a way that is disconnected from His will. This is why it is vital to seek the truth of God's Word, engage with sound biblical teaching, and allow our theology to be shaped by Scripture rather than culture or personal preferences.

Reflection Questions

1. How has your understanding of God been shaped by early teachings (e.g., Sunday School, Bible Study)? Where might you need to deepen or correct that understanding based on Scripture? (*Reflect on the roots of your faith and areas for growth.*)

2. What difference do you see between knowing about God and truly knowing God personally? (*Consider how relationship changes the way you experience Him.*)

3. When you think of God as the One who created everything, how does that deepen your relationship with Him?

4. In what ways has your theological understanding influenced your daily choices—such as family life, finances, entertainment, or social engagement? (*Trace the connection between belief and behavior.*)

5. How can being part of a faith community help you guard against misconceptions and deepen your relationship with God? (*Think about how community sharpens theology and discipleship.*)

Practical Exercises

1. Theology Foundations Journal:
   Write a personal statement answering: *Who is God to me?* Then, beside it, write what Scripture says about who God is (choose at least 3-5 verses). Compare and reflect on any differences.

2. Scripture Map Exercise:
   Read Genesis 1, John 1:1-18, and Hebrews 11 this week. Journal how each passage unveils a different aspect of God's nature (Creator, Spirit, Redeemer).

3. The "Broken GPS" Checkup:
   Identify one area of life (family, stewardship, relationships, social issues) where your decisions may be more influenced by culture than Scripture. Research what the Bible says about that area and plan one step of alignment.

4. Salvation Prayer Reflection:
   If you prayed (or renewed) the salvation prayer in this chapter, write a letter to yourself marking today's spiritual milestone. If you are already saved, write a letter reflecting on how that decision has shaped your journey with God.

5. Community Connection Commitment:
   Take one tangible step to engage deeper in a faith community this month: join a Bible study group, attend a midweek service, participate in a class, or find a mentor who can help sharpen your theology.

CHAPTER 2

Knowing His Nature, Trusting His Character

To truly know God, we must understand His nature and character. Scripture provides us with a clear picture of who He is—His love, justice, mercy, and holiness. These attributes define not only who God is but also how He engages with humanity.

God's Love

Frederick L. Ware (2008) asserts that "God's love is demonstrated through acts of liberation and empowerment, reflecting a divine commitment to the well-being and flourishing of oppressed communities" (p. 45). His love is not merely an emotion or a sentiment; it is an active force, working toward justice, restoration, and redemption. Throughout Scripture, God's love is displayed in transformative ways, culminating in the ultimate act of love—sending Jesus Christ to redeem humanity.

Perhaps the most well-known and profound expression of God's love is found in John 3:16 (NIV): "For God so loved the world that he gave his one and only Son, that whoever believes in him shall not perish but have eternal life." This verse reveals that, for God, love is not passive—it is active. Love moves, acts, gives, creates, and restores for the benefit of its object. In God's perspective, love is not just a feeling; it is a force that brings about transformation.

If we are to truly know God, we must understand His love as both active and unconditional. His love is agápē—freely given, without prerequisites or conditions. This truth can be difficult for many to grasp because, in our human relationships, love is often transactional, based on merit, reciprocity, or circumstance. Yet, God's love defies human standards. It is given without limit, beyond human worthiness, and remains steadfast regardless of our flaws.

Consider the magnitude of this love: God gave up His "one and only Son" for a world that had the agency to reject Him. He did not send Jesus to a righteous or redeemed people—He sent Him to a broken, sinful world, fully knowing that many would resist and refuse His perfect gift. And yet, He gave. That is love.

Paul echoes this truth in Romans 8:35-39, where he asks: "Who shall separate us from the love of Christ? Shall trouble or hardship or persecution or famine or nakedness or danger or sword?" After listing every conceivable trial, Paul concludes with a resounding declaration: nothing—no situation, no struggle, no force in heaven or on earth—can separate us from the love of God in Christ Jesus. His love is unbreakable, unshakable, and unrelenting.

In God's redemptive plan, salvation and eternal life are not forced upon humanity; they are freely offered. He leaves the decision to the individual, extending His love and inviting all to simply believe in Jesus Christ to be reconciled with Him. Jeremiah 31:3 (NIV) affirms this truth: "I have loved you with an everlasting love; I have drawn you with unfailing kindness." This is a love that does not wane, does not fade, and does not cease—even in the face of our mistakes, failures, or rebellion.

To truly know God is to understand His position on love: it is eternal, it is active, and it is given in boundless measure—covering, restoring, and redeeming all who receive it.

God's Justice

Frederick L. Ware (2008) states that "justice is an essential aspect of God's character, ensuring the righteous and equitable treatment of all individuals" (p. 62). God's justice is evident in His concern for the suffering, His defense of the vulnerable, and His call for righteousness and systemic change. His justice ensures that evil does not go unpunished and that His people are called to act justly in their own lives.

At the heart of God's justice is His unwavering commitment to protect His people from harm and oppression. A perception of God as indifferent or disengaged from the well-being of His people is inaccurate. Scripture makes it clear that He is actively involved in the affairs of humanity. In Romans 8:31 (NIV), Paul declares, "If God is for us, who can be against us?" This is not a passive statement—it is a resounding affirmation that we are not alone. God is not distant; He is intimately involved in securing justice for His people. The passage continues in Romans 8:33 (NIV): "Who will bring any charge against those whom God has chosen? It is God who justifies."

God is the ultimate Judge, whose judgments are both righteous and unquestionable. As the omniscient and sovereign ruler, His justice is perfect balancing both righteousness and mercy. He does not sit idly by while His people are trampled under injustice. Instead, He acts decisively and in His perfect timing, intervening against oppression.

One of the greatest biblical demonstrations of God's justice is His triumphant deliverance of Israel from Egyptian oppression. God confronted Pharaoh and the corrupt system that enslaved His people, executing divine judgment through plagues and miraculous signs. Exodus 3:7-8 (NIV) records God's declaration:

"I have indeed seen the misery of my people in Egypt. I have heard them crying out because of their slave drivers, and I am concerned about their suffering. So, I have come down to rescue them from the hand of the Egyptians and to bring them up out of that land into a good and spacious land, a land flowing with milk and honey."

God did not ignore the cries of the oppressed. Instead, He raised up a deliverer, Moses, an unlikely leader, to confront Pharaoh and demand justice. Despite Pharaoh's resistance, God demonstrated His supremacy by bringing plagues upon Egypt, forcing the hand of the oppressor. His justice was further revealed in the miraculous parting of the Red Sea, creating an unexpected pathway to freedom. Exodus 14:21-22 (NIV) describes this powerful moment:

"Then Moses stretched out his hand over the sea, and all that night the Lord drove the sea back with a strong east wind and turned it into dry land. The waters were divided, and the Israelites went through the sea on dry ground, with a wall of water on their right and on their left."

In this defining moment, God's justice prevailed. He defied natural laws, dismantled oppressive power structures, and led His people to freedom. And He is still the God of justice today.

God's justice is not confined to ancient history. He continues to raise up individuals to be voices for justice in the midst of oppression. He does not endorse racism, discrimination, sexism, ableism, or any form of systemic injustice. Proverbs 31:8-9 (NIV) commands, "Speak up for those who cannot speak for themselves, for the rights of all who are destitute. Speak up and judge fairly; defend the rights of the poor and needy."

God does not support systems that perpetuate greed, force food insecurity, inhumane housing conditions, or the dehumanization of others. Instead, He calls His people to act as instruments of justice, advocating for righteousness and fairness in every aspect of society.

One of the most profound demonstrations of God's justice and unity is found in Acts 2, on the Day of Pentecost. The Holy Spirit fell upon a diverse crowd from various regions, speaking different languages, yet they all understood one another. Acts 2:6 (NIV) states, "When they heard this sound, a crowd came together in bewilderment, because each one heard their own language being spoken."

This moment symbolizes the breaking down of barriers—cultural, racial, and linguistic—through the power of the Holy Spirit. Pentecost was not just a spiritual event; it was a declaration of God's vision for a unified, just, and inclusive kingdom. The justice of God does not divide—it unites.

God's Mercy

Frederick L. Ware (2008) describes God's mercy as "the means by which individuals experience forgiveness and restoration, demonstrating God's compassionate nature and His desire for reconciliation with humanity" (p. 78). Mercy is the bridge between justice and grace, making redemption possible. Through Christ, we witness the perfect union of these attributes—where sin is acknowledged, yet grace is extended.

For many, the concept of divine mercy is difficult to grasp because human mercy is often conditional and inconsistent. In our daily lives, mercy from others can be rare, but God's mercy is unwavering, restorative, and freely given. Psalm 103:8-10 (NIV) affirms this truth: "The Lord is compassionate and gracious, slow to anger, abounding in love. He will not always accuse, nor will he harbor his anger forever; he does not treat us as our sins deserve or repay us according to our iniquities." God's mercy is not based on our merit but on His character. Even though His holiness demands justice, He extends mercy to those who seek Him.

The redemption story is one of the greatest demonstrations of divine mercy. Because God is holy, His tolerance for sin is absolute—yet, in His mercy, He provides a remedy. Romans 5:8 (NIV) declares: "But God demonstrates his own love for us in this: While we were still sinners, Christ died for us."

Through Christ's sacrifice, we are reconnected with God and experience His unfailing love. This is not just a one-time act of mercy; it is an ongoing invitation for reconciliation. 1 John 1:9 (NIV) assures us: "If we confess our sins, he is faithful and just and will forgive us our sins and purify us from all unrighteousness." This daily mercy is a testament to God's enduring faithfulness.

The God of Holiness

Holiness is one of the defining attributes of God, setting Him apart from all that is sinful and impure. Frederick L. Ware (2008) explains that "holiness signifies God's moral purity and separateness from sin" (p. 91). As believers, we are called to reflect this holiness in our lives, not as a superficial display of righteousness, but as a deep and transformative work of God within us.

God's call to holiness is not about religious obligation; it is an invitation to spiritual maturity and a closer relationship with Him. 1 Peter 1:15-16 reminds us: "But just as he who called you is holy, so be holy in all you do; for it is written: 'Be holy, because I am holy.'" Holiness is a way of life that sets the believer apart, not by outward appearance alone, but through the inward work of the Holy Spirit.

The Holy Spirit plays a crucial role in shaping our character, aligning our desires with God's, and convicting us when we stray from His path. Holiness is a work that God accomplishes in us through His Spirit. It requires our participation in spiritual disciplines, such as prayer, fasting, and meditating on God's Word, that allow the Spirit to cultivate holiness in us.

Imagine someone painting a picture of you without ever meeting you. They gather descriptions from others, but when you finally see the portrait, it looks nothing like you. This is what happens when people define God based on opinions rather than Scripture. Many people have a distorted view of God—one shaped by culture, tradition, or personal biases rather than biblical truth.

Biblical Connection

In Exodus 34:6-7, Moses asks to see God's glory. In response, God reveals His nature: "The Lord, the Lord, the compassionate and gracious God, slow to anger, abounding in love and faithfulness, maintaining love to thousands, and forgiving wickedness, rebellion, and sin."

God did not merely describe Himself in abstract terms; He demonstrated His character through His actions. His love, justice, mercy, and holiness define how He interacts with His people. If we are to truly know God, we must seek to understand these attributes—not through opinion, but through His Word.

As we continue this journey, let us commit to knowing God as He has revealed Himself—grounding our theology and understanding in the truth of Scripture. The more we learn about Him, the more we are drawn into personal and intimate relationship with Him—rooted in His attributes and character. See God as He declares Himself in His Word. Know Him—not just by what you've heard, but by who He truly is.

Reflection Questions

1. Which of God's attributes—love, justice, mercy, or holiness—do you feel most connected to right now? Why? (Reflect on how your current season of life shapes your experience of God.)

2. How does understanding God's love as active and unconditional challenge or encourage your view of relationships with others? (Consider where your understanding of love needs to shift closer to God's model.)

3. In what ways have you personally witnessed God's justice—either in your life or in the world around you? (Think about moments where you saw God's protection, deliverance, or advocacy.)

4. How does experiencing God's mercy affect the way you extend mercy to others? (Reflect on how receiving mercy changes your ability to give it.)

5. Where is God inviting you into a deeper pursuit of holiness in your daily life? (Identify specific attitudes, habits, or relationships where the Spirit may be calling for growth.)

Practical Application Exercises

1. Attribute Study Journal:
    Choose one attribute of God (love, justice, mercy, or holiness) each week for the next month. Study related Scriptures and write a daily reflection on how you see that attribute showing up in your life or in the world.

2. Love in Action Challenge:
    Practice *active love* by intentionally serving someone without expecting anything in return this week. Document how it felt and what God showed you about His love through the experience.

3. Justice Advocacy Step:
    Identify one area of injustice (local or global) and commit to one act of advocacy—whether it's prayer, giving, learning more, or volunteering—to partner with God's heart for justice.

4. Mercy Extension Exercise:
    Think of one person who has wronged or disappointed you. Spend time praying for them daily for a week, asking God to help you extend mercy as He has shown you.

5. Holiness Audit:
    Set aside a day to prayerfully review your daily habits, language, entertainment, and relationships. Ask the Holy Spirit to reveal anything that needs realignment to reflect God's holiness—and commit to one change you can start making immediately.

CHAPTER 3

Removing Spiritual Blind Spots

magine a man who has worn the wrong prescription glasses for years. He assumes the world is supposed to look dull, blurry, and distorted. But the day he puts on the correct lenses, everything changes. Colors become vibrant. Details come into sharp focus. Reality, once blurred, becomes beautifully clear.

Many people experience God this way. They view Him through distorted lenses—shaped by pain, culture, misinformation, or even deliberate deception. These misconceptions prevent them from seeing God's true nature. But when they encounter Him as He truly is, their vision shifts—and clarity comes.

The Danger of Faulty Perception

Proverbs 14:12 (NIV) warns: "There is a way that appears to be right, but in the end it leads to death." Faulty knowledge about God doesn't just mislead—it can destroy. Misconceptions are more than innocent mistakes; they create barriers that keep us from experiencing the fullness of His love, grace, and truth.

Thankfully, God does not leave us to define Him through human opinion. In Exodus 34:6–7 (NIV), He proclaims: "The Lord, the Lord, the compassionate and gracious God, slow to anger, abounding in love and faithfulness…"

He reveals Himself clearly. Our role is to seek Him as He is—not as we assume Him to be. Isaiah 55:8–9 (NIV) reminds us: "For my thoughts are not your thoughts, neither are your ways my ways, declares the Lord."

Spiritual blindness is still a very real threat in our time. As 2 Corinthians 4:4 (NIV) states, *"The god of this age has blinded the minds of unbelievers, so that they cannot see the light of the gospel that displays the glory of Christ."*

Misconceptions about God create blind spots in our spiritual vision. They distort our understanding of His character and His will, keeping us from fully experiencing the truth of who He is.

Common Misconceptions About God

Throughout history, many have embraced distorted views of God. Let's confront some of these lies with the light of Scripture.

"God Does Not Hear the Prayers of Sinners"

If God didn't hear sinners, no one could ever repent. 1 John 1:9 (NIV) assures us: "If we confess our sins, he is faithful and just and will forgive us our sins and purify us from all unrighteousness."

God listens to the repentant heart. His ears are open to those who seek Him.

"God Endorses the Oppression of People"

This devastating lie has justified atrocities like slavery and injustice. But God is a God of justice. Isaiah 1:17 (NIV) commands: "Learn to do right; seek justice. Defend the oppressed." God stands with the oppressed. Misusing Scripture to justify injustice does not change His heart.

"God Is Indifferent to the Environment"

Some believe God is unconcerned with creation, but from the beginning, He appointed humanity as stewards of the earth. Environmental stewardship is a sacred trust given by God.

Genesis 2:15 (NIV) says: "The Lord God took the man and put him in the Garden of Eden to work it and take care of it."

"If I Follow God, My Life Will Be Easy"

Jesus was clear. John 16:33 (NIV) says: "In this world you will have trouble. But take heart! I have overcome the world."

Following Christ means facing trials, but it also means knowing we are never alone. Hardship refines our faith and draws us closer to Him.

"God Is Too Loving to Judge Anyone"

Yes, God is love (1 John 4:8), but His love does not cancel His justice. Isaiah 1:16–20 (NIV) calls us to repentance and righteousness, promising blessing for obedience and warning of consequences for rebellion.

God's discipline is a sign of His love, not a contradiction of it. Hebrews 12:6 (NIV) says: "The Lord disciplines the one he loves, and he chastens everyone he accepts as his son."

Seeing Clearly: Aligning Our Vision with God's Truth

Removing spiritual blind spots takes humility. We must allow Scripture—not assumptions—to shape our understanding of God. When we view Him through His truth, distorted perceptions fall away.

Just like the man who finally puts on the correct glasses, we begin to see God in His beauty, power, justice, and compassion. We come to know Him—not just in theory, but in truth.

As you continue on this journey, open your heart fully. Don't settle for second-hand beliefs or inherited assumptions. Seek the God who longs to reveal Himself to you personally. One of the most liberating experiences in this walk is seeing God as He truly is—not through the lens of human opinion, but through the truth of His Word. Every relationship thrives when it's built on truth—and your relationship with God is no different. If you truly want to know Him more, begin by replacing misconceptions with the truth of who He says He is.

Reflection Questions

1. How would you explain the difference between knowing about God intellectually and experiencing God personally?

2. What factors (upbringing, culture, experiences) have shaped your view of God? How do these align—or conflict—with Scripture?

3. Why do people create false images of God, and how can we guard against it?

4. How has your understanding of God changed over time? What experiences helped you grow?

5. Why is it important to continue seeking a deeper knowledge of God, rather than assuming we already know enough?

Practical Exercises

1. List 5–7 names or attributes of God (e.g., Jehovah Jireh – The Lord My Provider). Reflect on how each has been revealed in your life.

2. Spend a week meditating on Jeremiah 9:23–24. Journal daily about what God shows you.

3. Choose a biblical figure (e.g., Moses, David, Paul) and study how they pursued God. Reflect on what you can learn from their journey.

4. Each morning, pray: "Lord, help me know You beyond what I've been taught. Reveal Yourself to me in new ways."

CHAPTER 4

Beyond the Encounter

Many people have had encounters with God—powerful moments where they've felt His presence, witnessed His power, or heard His voice. But an encounter alone is not the goal. God desires more than a moment; He calls us into a relationship—one that is personal, daily, and life-changing.

Too often, we settle for distant admiration rather than deep connection. We hear others' testimonies, experience glimpses of God's power during worship, or feel His nearness in a time of crisis, but we fail to cultivate a lasting relationship beyond those moments. God wants more for us. He invites us to know Him personally, intimately, and continuously.

This chapter is an invitation to move beyond occasional encounters and step into a living, breathing relationship with God. It's about learning to recognize His voice in everyday life, experiencing His presence in both the ordinary and the extraordinary, and realizing that He is not just a God to be known from afar—He is a Father who longs for closeness with His children.

Beyond Knowledge: From Awareness to Relationship

We pause here to recognize a critical truth: simply knowing about God—understanding facts, quoting Scriptures, engaging in study—is only the beginning. A true relationship with Him through Jesus Christ requires something deeper.

If we limit our understanding of God to knowledge alone, we reduce Him to a historical figure—someone to study but not to experience. When God becomes only an object of study, we risk keeping Him at a distance, admiring Him like a celebrity rather than walking closely with Him as our Father.

But Scripture calls us higher. Jesus declared in John 17:3 (NIV): "Now this is eternal life: that they know you, the only true God, and Jesus Christ, whom you have sent."

This "knowing" is not intellectual alone; it is relational, experiential, and transformative. Psalm 34:8 (NIV) invites us: "Taste and see that the Lord is good; blessed is the one who takes refuge in him." God calls us not just to learn about His goodness but to experience it firsthand.

Our journey with God is meant to be dynamic, evolving, and deeply personal. As we seek Him, He promises to reveal Himself. Jeremiah 29:13 (NIV) affirms: "You will seek me and find me when you seek me with all your heart." The goal is not merely to study God but to walk with Him, not merely to observe His works but to participate in them. To know of Him is good—but to know Him is life-changing.

The Power of Divine Encounters: How Meeting God Changes Everything

Throughout Scripture, divine encounters transformed the lives of those who experienced them. These moments with God were not random; they were intentional, personal, and life-altering.

One of the most profound examples is the story of the Samaritan woman at the well. Her encounter with Jesus reveals powerful truths about how Christ meets us where we are, challenges our perceptions, and calls us into deeper relationship.

Jesus' decision to meet this woman was unconventional and bold. As a Jewish man, speaking to a Samaritan woman in public defied every societal norm. Yet Jesus intentionally positioned Himself for this encounter, demonstrating that God will cross every barrier—cultural, racial, gendered—to reach those He loves.

Some encounters with Christ are initiated by Him. He orchestrates moments in our lives to reveal Himself, inviting us into deeper intimacy, not just intellectual understanding.

When Jesus spoke to her, it began with a simple request for water. Yet quickly, the conversation moved beyond physical thirst. Jesus started tearing down the cultural, religious, and personal barriers that kept this woman bound.

In our encounters with Christ, He often does the same. He challenges mindsets, dismantles traditions, and corrects misconceptions that hinder our growth. True encounters with Jesus will always stretch us, calling us to see beyond our comfort zones.

One of the first barriers Jesus shattered was the idea that spiritual conversations were only for the "qualified." He made it clear that God speaks to whomever He chooses—regardless of gender, background, or social status. God is not distant or selective; He is present, willing, and ready to engage with anyone, in any condition. The truth is, one encounter with Jesus can change everything—your perspective, your desires, your focus, your vision, even the entire direction of your life. So pursue the real thing. Don't settle for surface-level or traditional rituals. Seek an authentic, transparent encounter with God—one that leaves a lasting imprint on your soul.

The Shift from Practical to Spiritual

As Jesus and the woman at the well spoke, Jesus introduced the concept of "living water." Yet the woman, thinking practically, could only imagine the physical well before her.

This teaches us something important: divine encounters lift our understanding from the natural to the spiritual. Jesus always points to realities greater than what we can see.

When Jesus asked the woman in John 4:16–19 to bring her husband, it wasn't to expose or shame her—it was to lovingly reveal that He already knew her story. He saw her brokenness, her past, and her hidden wounds—and still, He chose to engage her.

A true encounter with Christ is never shallow. He knows every detail of who we are, yet He moves toward us—not away—with grace, healing, and an invitation to relationship.

That's why we can come to Jesus just as we are—no masks, no filters, no pretending. He already knows everything about us, and still, He chooses us. So, bring your full, unedited self into His presence. The real you is the one He's after. And it's the real you that needs a real encounter—one that transforms you from the inside out.

A Revelation About Worship

As the conversation deepened, the woman raised a theological debate in John 4:20-23- Where should worship happen, Jerusalem or the Samaritan Mountain?

Jesus answered with a profound shift: "A time is coming and has now come when the true worshipers will worship the Father in the Spirit and in truth, for they are the kind of worshipers the Father seeks." -(John 4:23, NIV)

Through this moment, Jesus revealed that worship isn't about a location—it's about the posture of the heart. True worship isn't confined to temples, traditions, or rituals; it's rooted in spirit and truth.

Divine encounters often correct and reset our understanding of worship. They draw us out of routine and into real connection with the living God. Sometimes, Jesus meets us in worship just to clear away the misconceptions we've carried—ideas shaped more by tradition than truth.

To the woman at the well, Jesus made it clear: what matters most in worship is not the place, the method, or the timing—but the **who**. Worship is about God Himself. When you truly grasp that, you'll understand that God expects worship everywhere— from anyone whose heart is open. And that kind of worship flows from an authentic encounter with Him.

A Transformed Witness

When you approach God with intentionality and a genuine desire for encounter, transformation becomes possible—real transformation. Not just an emotional high, but a change so evident that even those around you will take notice.

The Samaritan woman experienced just that. By the end of her conversation with Jesus, everything changed. She left her water jar behind—a powerful, symbolic gesture that what she received was far greater than what she came for.

She ran back to her town and shared her encounter, saying: *"Come, see a man who told me everything I ever did. Could this be the Messiah?"* -(John 4:29, NIV)

Don't miss this: she left something behind. Every authentic encounter with Christ results in something being left on the altar—old habits, shame, distractions, even misguided expectations. What do you need to leave behind?

But it didn't stop there. Her testimony sparked faith in others. Her private encounter became a public movement. That's what a real encounter does—it ignites purpose. It gives birth to vision, reveals calling, and clarifies identity. The more you know Him, the more you begin to discover who you are in Him.

Encounters with God are not meant to end with us. They are seeds of transformation—planted in our lives, but intended to grow in the lives of others.

The Impact of a Divine Encounter

The Samaritan woman's story teaches us that an encounter with Jesus can:
- Break barriers that society or religion have built.
- Elevate our perspective from the natural to the spiritual.

- Reveal truth about ourselves while assuring us of God's unwavering love.
- Correct misconceptions about God, worship, and faith.
- Ignite a desire to testify and bring others to Christ.
- When we truly encounter Jesus, we are never the same.

Just as the Samaritan woman's testimony impacted her entire community, your encounter with God has the power to influence lives far beyond your own. It can send ripples of transformation that echo through families, communities—even generations.

Encountering Jesus isn't just about gaining knowledge; it's about being changed. And once we truly experience Him, we'll never see life the same way again.

Lord, help us to experience You more deeply. Let every encounter draw us closer to You and reveal more of who You are—and who we are in You. Amen.

Reflection Questions

1. Have you been living off past encounters with God or are you actively culti-vating a daily relationship with Him now? (Reflect on whether your connec-tion to God feels historical or living.)

2. What barriers—cultural, personal, or spiritual—might be standing between you and a deeper relationship with Christ? (Consider areas where God may be inviting you to let Him cross over and heal.)

3. How has God used an encounter in your life to reveal a deeper truth about yourself or your purpose? (Think about moments where He lovingly exposed something hidden to bring growth.)

4. In what ways has your understanding of worship been reshaped by personal encounters with God? (Reflect on how worship has moved beyond ritual or place for you.)

5. Are you sharing your encounters with Christ with others, or keeping them private? Why or why not? (Examine what holds you back or what motivates you to testify.)

Application Exercises

1. Encounter Testimony Journal:
    Write a detailed testimony about a personal encounter you've had with God. Focus not just on what happened, but how it changed you—and who else might need to hear it.

2. Barrier Breakthrough Exercise:
    Identify one "barrier" in your life (fear, shame, cultural mindset, etc.) and prayerfully ask God to begin tearing it down. Journal any insights or small victories as you surrender it to Him.

3. Worship Reset Challenge:
    Spend one week intentionally worshiping God outside of traditional settings—at home, during a walk, while driving. Focus on worshiping *in spirit and in truth*, not just in routine or tradition.

4. Living Water Meditation:
    Each morning for one week, meditate on John 4:13-14. Invite the Holy Spirit to reveal areas where you have been spiritually "thirsty" and ask Him to fill you with His living water.

5. Invite Others to Encounter:
    Choose one person this week with whom you can share part of your journey with Christ. It doesn't have to be formal—just an honest conversation about what it means to experience God personally.

CHAPTER 5

Faith That Invokes an Encounter

(Mark 5:25–34)

After suffering for twelve long years, the woman with the issue of blood reached out in faith—and Jesus acknowledged her personally. Her encounter led to healing and restoration, revealing several powerful principles about spiritual encounters with Christ. Moments like these move us beyond mere intellectual awareness into the realm of experiential transformation.

Unlike the Samaritan woman at the well, whose encounter was initiated by Jesus, this woman took the initiative. Mark, known for his vivid and fast-paced storytelling, places this event while Jesus was on His way to Jairus' house to heal a dying daughter. But along the way, His schedule was interrupted by a woman burdened by trauma, disappointment, and pain.

For twelve years, she had suffered—not only from the physical affliction of constant bleeding but also from the emotional and social consequences that came with it. She had been labeled unclean, shunned by society, met with rolling eyes, hushed whispers, and the cruel reality of isolation from communal worship and relationships. She had exhausted all of her resources, sought every remedy, and had only grown worse.

This woman was desperate—for healing, for change, for an encounter with the living God.

Some encounters with Christ are not initiated by Him. Sometimes, we must actively seek Him out for ourselves. This woman saw Jesus as the answer to her circumstances, despite the risks, the cultural barriers, and the religious restrictions that stood in her way.

She leaned into the tension of the moment, weighing the consequences of her actions. She knew she could be shunned, ridiculed, or even punished for daring to enter the crowd in her condition. Yet she made a bold decision: she was not leaving without at least trying to reach Jesus.

Life has a way of throwing curveballs—some devastating, some that leave us broken and desperate. But when we find ourselves in those moments, we must ask: Are we willing to push past every obstacle for an encounter with Jesus?

Her story reminds us: you don't have to wait for a religious gathering, a special prayer service, or a public invitation to engage Christ. You can invoke an encounter with Him simply by reaching out in faith.

Pushing Through for an Encounter

This woman didn't just come with faith—she came with a plan. She had already determined in her heart that she would reach out and touch Jesus, believing that even touching the hem of His garment would be enough to heal her.

Are you willing to take the risk of pushing past the noise—the religious critics, the societal expectations, and the doubters—just to have a real encounter with Jesus? For one woman, it was risky, yet deeply intimate. With a single touch, she expressed faith, desperation, and trust—all at once. And Jesus responded.

Her faith wasn't passive—it was active. She had to press through. And sometimes, so do we. There are moments when you have to push past fear, shame, and resistance just to get into His presence.

Take a lesson from this woman: don't stop at belief—**push**. Push through until you touch Him. That's where the encounter happens.

She had to push through the crowds pressing around Him. She had to push through the whispers of condemnation. She had to push through the trauma of her past memories. She had to push through the fear of rejection. She had to push through society's barriers that labeled her an outcast. She had to push through her own internal doubts and fears.

She had already decided—it was worth the cost. What about you? Do you desire an encounter with Jesus enough to push past the obstacles in your way? I pray your answer is yes. Because passivity won't lead you into sacred moments. Sometimes, you have to move. You have to press in. It's in that bold step of faith that intimacy with Christ is found.

Some life circumstances make it harder to reach for Jesus. At times, voices—whether from others or from within—whisper things like: You're not worthy. What if nothing changes? You've tried before and failed—why try again? You've prayed, and it didn't seem to make a difference.

Yet this woman refused to let fear or failure have the final word. She pushed through it all, believing that despite the odds and the opposition, Jesus could and would respond to her faith and grant her an intimate healing even in a crowded space.

Faith That Moves Jesus

An encounter with Christ intensifies when you bring faith to the table. This woman didn't approach Jesus with wishful thinking; she brought the kind of active, confident faith that pleases God.

> "Now faith is confidence in what we hope for and assurance about what we do not see."
>
> — Hebrews 11:1, NIV

Jesus responds to faith. He is drawn to it. Faith moves His heart, and He delights in seeing it displayed.

> The woman's faith led her to reach out—and immediately, she was healed. But Jesus didn't allow her to slip away unnoticed. He stopped, turned, and asked, "Who touched me?"
>
> — Mark 5:30

His disciples were confused. After all, the crowd was pressing around Him. How could He single out one touch? Because this was no accidental bump—this was intentional faith reaching for Him. When the woman, trembling, came forward to confess, Jesus did not scold her. He reassured her with words that transformed her identity: "Daughter, your faith has healed you. Go in peace and be freed from your suffering." (Mark 5:34) In that moment, she wasn't just a woman with an issue—she became a beloved daughter healed by the Son of the living God.

From Knowledge to Praxis: Living Out Your Faith

This encounter shows us that faith is not merely something we believe intellectually; it is something we live out. Many of us know the Scriptures, hear the sermons, and memorize the promises of God. But faith is more than knowledge. It requires action.

This woman didn't just believe Jesus could heal—she acted on that belief. She moved her body, pressed through obstacles, and extended her hand.

When faith moves into action, it ushers in miracles, signs, and wonders. "Faith without works is dead." (James 2:26)

This is what it means to move from head knowledge to heart encounter. Knowing about Jesus is a start—but experiencing Him will transform everything. And it all begins with faith.

The Power of a Determined Encounter

The woman's story teaches us several powerful truths about encountering Christ:

- Some encounters require pursuit.
- There are moments when we must take the first step toward Jesus.
- Faith requires action.
- Hope alone is not enough; we must move forward with confidence in His power.
- Barriers must be pushed through.
- Doubts, fears, past trauma, and societal restrictions must not keep us from Christ.
- Jesus responds to faith.
- When we reach out with determined belief, He acknowledges it and moves toward us.
- Encounters with Jesus bring total restoration. He didn't just heal her body— He gave her peace and called her "daughter."

Are You Ready to Reach for Him? This woman risked everything to touch Jesus. What about you? Are you willing to push past the obstacles to get into His presence? Are you ready to turn what you know into what you do?

Jesus is not just looking for those who admire Him from a distance. He's looking for those willing to reach out in faith, believing He will meet them there. Your faith has the power to invoke an encounter with Jesus- God in the flesh. Will you reach for God today?

Reflection Questions

1. When you think about faith leading to an encounter with God, what biblical examples come to mind—and how do they inspire you? (Reflect on people like the woman with the issue of blood, blind Bartimaeus, or others.)

2. Have you ever experienced a moment where your bold step of faith resulted in a clear encounter with God? (Describe what happened and how it impacted your relationship with Him.)

3. What fears or doubts most often keep you from stepping out in the kind of faith that invites God's movement? (Be honest about internal struggles that can silence courageous faith.)

4. How do you balance waiting on God's timing with actively exercising faith that expects Him to move? (Reflect on the tension between patience and persistence.)

5. What would change in your life if you truly believed that your faith could invoke a fresh encounter with God today? (Imagine how your prayers, your actions, and your expectations would shift.)

Application Exercises

1. Bold Prayer Challenge:
    Write out three bold, specific prayers—requests that require real faith to be-lieve for. Pray over them daily for one week, believing God for an encounter in response to your faith.

2. Faith Encounter Journal:
    Start a journal specifically to record moments when your faith has resulted in a fresh experience of God's presence, provision, or peace. Revisit it often to build your expectation.

3. Identify Your Faith Barriers:
    Write down two areas where fear, doubt, or discouragement have limited your faith. Next to each, write a scripture promise to replace the fear with truth (e.g., Mark 11:24, Hebrews 11:6).

4. Step Out Exercise:
    Do one thing this week that stretches your faith—whether it's sharing your testimony, giving generously, praying for someone openly, or starting a project God placed on your heart.

5. Faith Confession Practice:
    Each morning for seven days, declare out loud:
    "God responds to my faith. I trust You to meet me today. I am expecting an encounter with You." Watch how your mindset and heart shift as you cultivate expectancy.

CHAPTER 6

Dwell and Remain in His Presence

"Whoever dwells in the shelter of the Most High will rest in the shadow of the Almighty."

— Psalm 91:1, NIV

"Remain in me, as I also remain in you. No branch can bear fruit by itself."

— John 15:4–5, NIV

At the heart of both of these passages is an invitation—a call to consistency, commitment, and an ongoing presence with the Lord. To dwell is not to visit occasionally or pass through in moments of convenience. It is to abide. To stay. To linger intentionally in communion with Him.

One of the hallmarks of maturity—whether in institutions, relationships, or spiritual life—is consistency. True consistency is not about mechanical repetition; it's about steady, growing engagement. It's about deepening intimacy over time through meaningful encounters.

Consider marriage. The early years often present challenges, as two individuals learn to blend lives, dreams, and differences. Yet, with good tools, consistent nurturing, and intentional love, marriage blossoms into something beautiful—rich with history, meaning, and trust.

This is the very picture God desires with us: a loving, meaningful, and intimate relationship. Consistency in dwelling in His presence is key.

We find His presence through many doorways—worship, Scripture reading, meditation, reflection on His works, prayer, and simple conversation with the Lord. Each of these spiritual practices is a path into His manifested presence. The objective is to engage them consistently, to meet Him there, and to remain.

Consistency, however, requires commitment—the kind of commitment that keeps an agreement without wavering. True commitment grows out of appreciation, loyalty, connection, and a deep inner desire.

I remember times when I served faithfully under church leaders, motivated by a deep appreciation for what they had done for me. That sense of loyalty fueled my desire to meet expectations, not out of obligation, but out of love and gratitude.

When we reflect on what Christ has done for us—the moments only we can testify about—it stirs a personal gratitude that deepens our commitment to Him.

Gratitude then gives birth to desire. And desire, depending on its focus, can either nourish a relationship or lead it astray. I'm advocating for a fierce, intense, thirsty desire for Christ.

Have you ever been so thirsty that you desperately searched for water? Your mouth dry, your energy fading, your body pleading for relief? That level of longing is exactly what Scripture describes when it says, "As the deer pants for streams of water, so my soul pants for you, my God." -(Psalm 42:1, NIV)

That spiritual thirst fuels commitment. It stokes the fire of consistency. And before you know it, you find yourself dwelling with Christ—not just at church on Sunday mornings, but in everyday moments. Walking, driving, resting, traveling by plane or train—you find yourself aware of Him, longing for Him, dwelling with Him.

Dwelling with Christ is not confined to a location; it's the life posture of a heart that seeks Him always.

In our human relationships, we naturally enjoy spending time with those who bring joy, encouragement, and belonging. Their presence meets a need deep within us. How much more should the presence of Jesus, who has rescued, restored, and renewed us, compel us to linger?

To know Christ more is to dwell with Him—through every season, in every moment.

Dwelling with Christ is not passive. It's active. It's transformative. It invites us to observe, absorb, learn, and experience Him in fresh ways. It means becoming aware of truths about Him we may have never considered before.

Through prayer, fasting, worship, praise, Scripture, and meditation, we are continually invited to dwell with Him. And with that dwelling come divine benefits:

- When we dwell in His presence, we find shelter and protection.
- We experience covering and guidance.
- We receive joy, rest, and renewal.
- We are given solace for weary days and strength for the journey ahead.

Acts 3:19 (NIV) promises: "Times of refreshing come from the presence of the Lord." And Jesus reiterates this in John 15:4–5 (NIV): "Remain in me, as I also remain in you. No branch can bear fruit by itself; it must remain in the vine. Neither can you bear fruit unless you remain in me. I am the vine; you are the branches. If you remain in me and I in you, you will bear much fruit; apart from me you can do nothing."

Jesus offers us a powerful image of connection and dependence. Isn't that what your soul longs for right now? A deeper connection—so real that you can sense you're not walking through life alone. So close that you can feel His presence entering your heart, detect the aroma of His nearness, and know without a doubt that He is with you.

This kind of connection cultivates a divine dependency—not out of weakness, but out of trust. It's a sacred intimacy that welcomes His presence and rejects self-sufficiency. This is what it means to know God more—intimacy birthed through intentional encounters.

Jesus illustrated it perfectly with the image of the vine and the branch. A branch only thrives by staying connected to the vine. Likewise, our spiritual vitality flows from staying connected to Christ. Without Him, we wither. But in Him, we flourish.

When we dwell with Him, we receive nourishment for our souls. We develop spiritual stability and endurance. We share in His strength and divine structure. We grow in our awareness of His will. We find the power to resist distractions that seek to pull us away.

To disconnect from Him is to deprive ourselves of the very life-giving flow that sustains us.

In both Psalm 91 and John 15, there is a divine whisper—a holy invitation to every soul who truly desires to know Him more.

Dwell. Remain.

Reflection Questions

1. What does it personally mean to you to "dwell" in God's presence rather than just visit occasionally? (Reflect on the difference between momentary experiences with God and ongoing communion.)

2. How would you describe the condition of your heart when you are consistently abiding in God's presence? (Think about the peace, strength, or sensitivity you experience—or lack.)

3. What are the biggest obstacles that keep you from remaining in His presence throughout your day? (Name specific distractions, busyness, or heart struggles.)

4. How does remaining in God's presence impact your relationships, your work, and your inner peace? (Notice how the "dwelling life" flows outward.)

5. What specific habits or rhythms help you cultivate a lifestyle of dwelling in God's presence? (Consider both spiritual disciplines and heart postures.)

Application Exercises

1. Scripture Meditation on Abiding:
    Spend 10 minutes each day for a week meditating on John 15:4-5. Slowly repeat the phrase: *"Remain in Me, and I will remain in you,"* letting it settle deeply into your spirit.

2. Create a Dwelling Space:
    Designate a specific place in your home (even just a chair or a corner) as your "dwelling spot"—a space where you intentionally meet with God daily for prayer, worship, or quietness.

3. Dwell Check-In:
    Set an alarm three times a day (morning, midday, evening) that simply reminds you to pause, breathe deeply, and whisper, *"Lord, I dwell in You."* Practice consciously re-centering yourself in His presence.

4. Presence Walks:
    Take a 15-minute walk outside with no phone, no music, no distractions. As you walk, whisper prayers of gratitude and listen for God's nearness in the stillness of creation.

5. Journal Your Remaining:
    Each evening for one week, write down ways you sensed God's presence during the day—and where you noticed yourself drifting. End each entry with a short prayer asking God to deepen your desire to stay close.

CHAPTER 7

A Deeper Desire to Know God in Suffering

Paul's words in Philippians 3:10 (NIV) express a longing that transcends superficial faith: "I want to know Christ—yes, to know the power of his resurrection and participation in his sufferings, becoming like him in his death."

This statement highlights both the highs and the lows of a relationship with Jesus. To truly know Him is not just to celebrate His victories, but to walk through the difficult moments with Him as well. Paul acknowledges that knowing Christ is not only about experiencing the triumph of the resurrection; it also requires embracing the painful path that led there.

Too often, we rush toward the victory—the breakthrough, the resurrection, the happy ending—without fully engaging in the struggle, the suffering, and the endurance required along the way. Yet deep relationships are not formed in moments of success alone, but in seasons of trial.

Think about it. Who cherishes friends who are only present during celebrations but vanish during grief? Who appreciates well-wishers who acknowledge injustice but refuse to stand alongside you in it? True companionship is demonstrated in the trenches—in the hard places, in the moments when pain is real and sacrifice is required.

A Willingness to Suffer

Paul didn't simply want to know Christ in His resurrection power. He wanted to participate in His sufferings.

That's a radical request unless you understand the depth of true companionship and commitment. To love someone deeply is to share in their pain, not just their glory.

Paul was saying, "I am willing to suffer for Christ's sake. I am not just here for the miraculous, the victories, and the celebrations—I am here for the hard journey too."

This perspective is what allowed him to say with unwavering confidence: "I have learned the secret of being content in any and every situation, whether well fed or hungry, whether living in plenty or in want" (Philippians 4:12, NIV).

Suffering is not an exception in the Christian walk; it is part of the journey. Jesus Himself prepared His disciples with these words: "If they persecuted me, they will persecute you also" - (John 15:20, NIV) and "In this world you will have trouble. But take heart! I have overcome the world" - (John 16:33, NIV).

To know God deeply, we must not avoid suffering, fear it, or attempt to maneuver around it. Instead, we are called to endure it when it comes, knowing that the suffering we face cannot compare to the glory that will be revealed in us -(Romans 8:18).

Jesus Knew Suffering — And So Will We

If we are to know Christ intimately, we must remember that He suffered profoundly.

- He knew grief, weeping at the tomb of Lazarus - (John 11:35).
- He knew rejection, as many from His own community turned their backs on Him - (John 1:11).
- He faced false accusations, enduring injustice, betrayal, and humiliation - (Matthew 26:59–67).
- He experienced physical pain, being beaten, crucified, and bearing the full weight of human sin - (Isaiah 53:3–5).

Yet, His suffering was never wasted. His pain carried divine purpose. And because of His endurance, we now have hope.

In 2 Timothy 2:12 (NIV), we are promised: "If we endure, we will also reign with him."

God does not call us to seek out suffering, nor does He delight in our pain. But when suffering comes—through life's hardships, persecutions, or trials—He calls us to endure as faithful soldiers - (2 Timothy 2:3).

Suffering is Temporary — But Glory is Eternal

Peter gives us this powerful encouragement: *"And after you have suffered a little while, the God of all grace, who has called you to his eternal glory in Christ, will himself restore, confirm, strengthen, and establish you"* - (1 Peter 5:10, ESV).

Suffering is not escapable—it's inevitable. But Peter reminds us that even suffering comes with a deadline. Though we may not know when that season will end, we trust the One who holds all time in His hands. He knows our limits, and He will not take us beyond what we can bear.

Peter challenges us to lift our expectations—not just to endure suffering, but to grow through it. There is another level of maturity, strength, and spiritual depth waiting on the other side. And beyond the trial lies a glory we can't yet imagine.

As believers, we must learn to embrace both the bitter and the sweet. Jesus Himself walked a path marked by suffering—socially, relationally, and physically. Instead of always trying to rebuke suffering, maybe we should seek the glory within it, since we must walk through it anyway.

Suffering is not the final chapter. It is part of the journey—a necessary road that shapes, purifies, and prepares us for the glory that lies ahead.

There is restoration coming.
There is strengthening ahead.
There is eternal glory awaiting those who hold fast to Christ.

To know Him fully means embracing both the cross and the crown. It means walking through both trials and triumphs. It means allowing both suffering and celebration to reveal the character of our Savior—and in the process, being shaped into His likeness.

When we choose to walk this road with Christ, we come to understand not just what He has done, but who He is.

Our Redeemer.
Our Companion.
Our Eternal King.

The Resurrection stands as the pinnacle of our Christian faith. But Christ's victory at Calvary wasn't just meant to be celebrated—it was meant to change us. Resurrection is not about tradition; it's about transformation. Not a temporary adjustment or a seasonal shift, but a deep, irreversible change—the kind of change Robert Quinn calls *deep change*.

True transformation doesn't come easily. It comes through pressing. Just as olives must be crushed to produce oil, God often leads us into our own Gethsemane moments—seasons of pressure where the Spirit draws us deeper. In those sacred places, God extracts something precious from us. Not to harm, but to refine. To produce oil. To birth anointing.

Gethsemane is personal. It's the place where you realize that God is your only source. And it is in that realization that true transformation begins—because pressure is what produces the oil.

Here's the truth: there are seasons when you must walk alone with God. The oil is personal. No one else can earn it for you.

Your Gethsemane season is your opportunity to be pressed, purified, and changed. It may sound strange—alone with God—but it's real. When no one else shows up, when friends fall asleep, when human support fails, God is still present in the press. And just like Jesus in Gethsemane, we must survive the pressing if we want the oil to flow from our lives.

Pressing Prepares You for the Pain of Disappointment

"Then Jesus went with his disciples to a place called Gethsemane, and he said to them, 'Sit here while I go over there and pray.' He took Peter and the two sons of Zebedee along with him, and he began to be sorrowful and troubled" - (Matthew 26:36–37, NIV).

Jesus was surrounded by His closest friends—and yet, when He needed them most, they could not stay awake. Gethsemane reveals who is really equipped to walk with you in the press. There is pain in realizing that even those closest to you have limits. There is heartbreak when those you've poured into cannot pour back into you. But hear this, their weakness is not necessarily a lack of love. It's a limitation of capacity.

God sometimes allows you to see people's limits—not to wound you, but to press you closer to Him.

The message is clear: to truly know God more, we must also know Him through the suffering and pressing of Jesus Christ. If our desire to know Him is genuine, then the process is not optional—it's essential.

Learning to Pray Under Pressure

"Going a little farther, he fell with his face to the ground and prayed, 'My Father, if it is possible, may this cup be taken from me. Yet not as I will, but as you will'" (Matthew 26:39, NIV).

Jesus prayed under pressure. He prayed while being crushed. He prayed through sorrow. And He prayed persistently—the same prayer three times.

Why? Because persistent prayer draws out the oil.

Learning to pray under pressure is one of the most powerful disciplines you will ever cultivate.

Pray when answers delay.
Pray when heaven seems silent.
Pray with focus.
Pray in faith.
Pray until the oil begins to flow.
Persistence is part of the pressing.

And remember—**in Gethsemane, heaven was silent**. But silence does not equal absence. God was still fully present in the pressing, in the crushing, in the agony of Christ. If you truly desire to know the depths of God and experience the fullness of His character, you must also learn to embrace His silence.

There will be moments when God is so quiet, it feels like you could hear a pin drop. But His silence is not neglect, nor is it punishment. It's sacred. It's intentional. It's what we might call **holy silence**—and sometimes, the most profound revelations come not in the noise, but in the stillness.

Knowing Him means trusting Him—**even when He says nothing.**

Sometimes, His silence is His way of saying: "I have already spoken. Now, trust and obey."

Obedience Is Kingdom Currency

"Rise! Let us go! Here comes my betrayer!"

— Matthew 26:46, NIV

Jesus submitted to the Father's will, not because the pain had vanished, but because the purpose had been revealed. Submission under pressure releases destiny.

Your obedience today is tied to someone else's breakthrough tomorrow. That's why surviving Gethsemane matters. You cannot bypass Gethsemane and still walk in real power. You cannot skip the pressing and still carry true anointing.

In Gethsemane, the situation did not change. Jesus changed. The mountain didn't move. But Jesus was moved to complete surrender.

When you survive your Gethsemane season, you may not see immediate external change—but you will feel deep internal transformation.

You will come out stronger.
Surrendered.
Anointed.
Ready.
Closer to Him.

As Hebrews 5:8 reminds us: "Though He was a Son, He learned obedience through what He suffered."

For the believer who is truly pursuing a deeper, more intimate knowledge of God, there comes a realization: obedience matters most in the midst of suffering. It is in these hard seasons that spiritual maturity takes root—not by escaping the pain, but by remaining faithful through it.

The truest companions are those who stay close in difficulty. And in the same way, our love for God is proven when we walk with Him—not just in joy, but also in sorrow.

May we grow in our obedience and be able to say with confidence: **"I now know Him more deeply—because I suffered with Him."**

Reflection Questions

1. How do you typically respond when you encounter seasons of suffering? (Do you tend to draw closer to God, pull away, or try to endure it on your own?)

2. What does the Garden of Gethsemane teach you about Jesus' humanity and His willingness to surrender? (Reflect on the tension between Christ's desire and His submission to the Father's will.)

3. Have you ever experienced a personal "Gethsemane moment" where you wrestled deeply with God's will? (Describe that experience and what it revealed about your relationship with God.)

4. In what ways has suffering either deepened or challenged your desire to know Christ more intimately? (Consider both the struggles and the spiritual growth that have come from painful seasons.)

5. What does it mean to you personally to say, "Not my will, but Yours be done"? (Think about areas of your life where surrender is still a struggle.)

Application Exercises

1. Gethsemane Reflection Prayer:
    Set aside 30 minutes this week to quietly reflect on Luke 22:39-46. Write your own prayer of surrender to God, expressing both your fears and your faith.

2. Suffering Story Journal:
    Write about a time when suffering brought unexpected spiritual growth. Identify what changed in your heart, your prayers, and your view of God through that experience.

3. Create a Surrender List:
    Make a list of three areas in your life where you are still holding on to control. Next to each one, write a prayer committing it into God's hands, following Christ's example in Gethsemane.

4. Companion in Suffering:
    Reach out to someone currently walking through a hard season. Offer to pray with them or simply listen. Becoming a "Gethsemane companion" for some-one else deepens your sensitivity to Christ's ministry of presence in suffering.

5. Daily "Not My Will" Reminder:
    For one week, begin each morning by verbally praying:

    "Father, today, not my will but Yours be done. Teach me to trust You more, even when it hurts."

    Track in a journal any ways God shifts your heart or leads you differently dur-ing the day.

CHAPTER 8

Recognizing God's Voice and Presence

Learning to Recognize a Loved One's Voice

A child can recognize their parent's voice even in the midst of a crowded, noisy room. This ability doesn't happen instantly—it comes from years of closeness, familiarity, and trust.

The same is true when it comes to recognizing God's voice. The more we spend time with Him, the clearer His voice becomes in our lives.

Jesus makes this truth clear in John 10:27 (NIV): "My sheep listen to my voice; I know them, and they follow me."

Did you hear Him? Did you recognize His voice? He is always speaking, but only those who belong to Him—those who are His sheep—can truly discern it.

As a parent, I am convinced that God has given us a unique ability to recognize the voice of our own children. Amidst all the shouts, cries, and laughter of other children, I could always pick out the voice of my own sons, especially when they were in distress. No matter how loud the environment was, I never failed to detect their voices—it was instinctual because they are my children.

Just as important as me knowing their voices was their ability to recognize mine. When they were afraid at night, just hearing the voice of their mother or father brought them peace, comfort, and security. The same is true for believers—if we are His sheep, we should be able to distinguish the voice of Christ above all others.

Jesus didn't just say, "My sheep hear my voice"—He also said, "I know them, and they follow me." There is a knowing, a listening, and a responding. To know Christ intimately is to be able to recognize His voice, even when other voices are louder, more persuasive, or confidently misleading.

How Do We Learn Christ's Voice?

The voice of Jesus is inseparable from His Word. He will never speak contrary to what has already been spoken and recorded in Scripture.

This is why knowing the Word of God is essential for every believer.

Psalm 119:11 (NIV) declares: "I have hidden your word in my heart that I might not sin against you."

The more Scripture we deposit into our hearts and minds, the better equipped we are to recognize His voice and discern whether something aligns with truth or contradicts it.

Jesus has already spoken many things to us:

"And surely I am with you always, to the very end of the age" (Matthew 28:20) — His presence is constant.

"Love your enemies and pray for those who persecute you" (Matthew 5:44) — His call to love is radical.

"Do to others as you would have them do to you" (Luke 6:31) — His words shape our character.

"Whatever you did for one of the least of these, you did for me" (Matthew 25:40) — His heart is for the marginalized.

"I have given you authority to trample on snakes and scorpions and to overcome all the power of the enemy" (Luke 10:19) — His power is within us.

The more we internalize His words, the more we will recognize when He is speaking.

Henry T. Blackaby, in his work *Hearing God's Voice*, beautifully underscores that God's guidance always aligns with Scripture and is personalized to our life situations. He writes, "When God speaks, he does not give new revelation about himself that contradicts what he has already revealed in Scripture. Rather, God speaks to give application of his Word to the specific circumstances in your life."

Discerning His Voice from the Imitator

Satan, the deceiver, knows how to manipulate words to sound like Jesus. From the very beginning in the Garden of Eden, he twisted God's words to deceive Eve (Genesis 3:1-4) even when he tempted Jesus in the wilderness, he misused Scripture to try to trick Him (Matthew 4:1-11).

The enemy will always attempt to distort truth just enough to sound almost right—but when we are continually learning what Christ has already said, we will be able to recognize what is truly from Jesus and what is not.

Can you hear Him?
Can you recognize the sweetness of His voice?

Knowing His voice is the key to knowing Him more.
Keep listening.
Keep dwelling in His Word.
His voice will become clearer with every passing day.

Hearing God's Voice Today

It is important to note that many people claim to hear the audible voice of God.

Although it is absolutely possible for God to communicate audibly if He so chooses, it is rare in this dispensation. More often, God speaks through His Word, through the Holy Spirit's nudging, through situations and circumstances, or through a deep internal knowing.

However, it is critical that any assertion of hearing from God must stand the test of examination by the Word of God. If what an individual claims to hear violates or contradicts Scripture, that "hearing" must be deemed in error.

God will never violate or speak contrary to His written Word. This is why it is so necessary to engage in constant and persistent Bible study. By immersing ourselves in Scripture, we not only learn God's written truth, but we become more familiar with His voice.

It is also imperative that believers are connected to a local assembly where the Word of God is taught faithfully and consistently. Community provides accountability, exhortation, and protection.

Beyond personal study and corporate worship, it is wise to seek the counsel of godly mentors, pastors, teachers, and trusted fellow believers. There is great safety in the multitude of godly counsel.

When you believe you have heard instruction from God, it is both healthy and wise to use the wisdom of others to help discern and confirm the message. God often uses the body of Christ to confirm His voice.

A Personal Example of Discerning His Voice

I have used this approach to discern the voice of the Lord in many instances throughout my life. One vivid example is when I reentered the military as a chaplain. I heard the Lord speak clearly through the Spirit, saying, "I have sent you to a mission field where you know the language and culture. I have sent you into the military to be a chaplain."

The sense of calling was undeniable—but even then, I knew it was necessary to seek wise counsel to ensure I had heard correctly.

I asked trusted leaders, mentors, and fellow believers to help me discern the voice of the Lord. After many conversations, confirmations, and prayerful consideration, including affirmation from my oldest son, Ephraim Amos Jackson, each one confirmed that the call was legitimate and aligned with God's will.

As a result, I entered the chaplaincy with great reassurance and confidence, knowing I had exhausted every means to discern the voice of the Lord.

There was a deep sense of relief and gratitude to have that affirmed reassurance—that God had spoken, and that I had discerned His voice appropriately.

Hearing God clearly and responding faithfully is not something we stumble into. It is cultivated intentionally—through His Word, through His Spirit, through community, and through practice.

As we grow in spiritual sensitivity, recognizing His voice becomes a natural response, just like a child who knows the sound of their father's voice in the middle of a crowd.

Keep leaning in.
Keep listening.
Keep learning.

He is speaking—and His sheep know His voice.

Reflection Questions

1. How have you experienced God's voice in your life up to this point? (Think about moments where you sensed His leading, even if it wasn't audible)

2. What distractions most often keep you from recognizing God's presence? (Identify internal or external barriers that compete for your spiritual attention)

3. When was the last time you felt certain that God was speaking to you? (Reflect on what circumstances surrounded that moment and how you responded)

4. How does your familiarity with Scripture impact your ability to recognize God's voice? (Consider the connection between knowing His Word and discerning His whispers)

5. What role does trust play in recognizing and responding to God's voice? (Examine how your level of trust in God influences your spiritual sensitivity)

Application Exercises

1.   Daily Quiet Time Challenge:
     Set aside 15 minutes each day for the next week to sit quietly with no agenda—just listening for God's voice after reading a short passage of Scripture (e.g., John 10:27).

2.   Distraction Audit:
     Create a list of the top five distractions in your life. For each one, write one practical step you can take to minimize its impact on your spiritual sensitivity.

3.   Voice Recognition Journaling:
     Begin a "Voice of God" journal. Each time you believe God is speaking to you—through Scripture, prayer, a person, or circumstances—write it down. Review it weekly to notice patterns.

4.   Scripture Meditation Exercise:
     Choose one verse about hearing God's voice (e.g., Isaiah 30:21). Meditate on it daily for one week, reading it slowly, praying it back to God, and writing what you sense He is saying to you.

5.   Spiritual Sensitivity Fast:
     Choose to fast from one thing (social media, TV, unnecessary conversations, etc.) for three days. During the time you would normally engage in that activity, intentionally seek God's presence in prayer or Scripture.

CHAPTER 9

Deepening Your Walk with God Through Prayer

"But Jesus often withdrew to lonely places and prayed."

— Luke 5:16 (NIV)

The willingness to communicate stands as one of the most personal and intimate expressions of relationship. Every strong connection is rooted in clear, honest, and authentic communication. When these elements are healthy, they serve as a catalyst, igniting a deeper intimacy between individuals.

Prayer is our divine means of communication with the Lord of Lords. Whether it is a humble cry, a feeble attempt to articulate our hearts, or an exuberant shout of joy and praise, the Father listens intently. What a blessing it is to know that the God who created heaven and earth delights in hearing from His children. Even more astounding is the truth that He responds back to us!

Friend, our prayers do not need to be eloquent or filled with fancy words to impress the Father. God is not moved by our vocabulary; He is moved by the sincerity of our hearts. The intent and authenticity behind our words matter more than the words themselves. And so, we must recognize that in prayer, posture matters.

The Posture Matters: How We Approach and With What Mindset

Daniel 6:10 (NIV) — "Now when Daniel learned that the decree had been published, he went home to his upstairs room where the windows opened toward Jerusalem. Three times a day he got down on his knees and prayed, giving thanks to his God, just as he had done before."

Posture is not just about our physical stance—it is about the position of our heart. How we approach the Father in prayer shapes the depth of our relationship with Him. Jesus modeled this for us, often withdrawing to lonely, quiet places to pray. Daniel demonstrated it too, continuing in prayer despite facing the threat of the lion's den.

Much like we were taught as children to say, "Yes ma'am" or "No sir" out of respect, we approach God with awe, wonder, respect, and reverence. Yet, our approach should never be so formal that it becomes rigid or inauthentic. Prayer is not about performance; it's about presence.

When preparing to pray, it's important to find a space conducive to real, honest communication. It might be by a riverbank, in your car, or even in your bathroom. Jesus understood that environment matters—some spaces are filled with distractions that can pull us away from fully engaging with the Father. Seek a place where your heart can be open and your mind focused.

Equally important is the when of prayer. Choose times when you are most alert, thoughtful, and engaged—not when you are sleepy, distracted, or preoccupied. Give God your best moments, not your leftover ones. Of course, life will sometimes thrust us into urgent prayer at inopportune times—and God welcomes those cries, too. The key is to stay mindful and responsive to the Spirit's leading.

Ultimately, prayer demands a posture of humility and gratefulness—a deep reverence that the Almighty would even entertain our conversation. The way we approach Him shapes how we experience Him.

What to Say: The Content of Prayer

Matthew 6:9-13 (NIV) — "This, then, is how you should pray: 'Our Father in heaven, hallowed be your name, your kingdom come, your will be done, on earth as it is in heaven. Give us today our daily bread. And forgive us our debts, as we also have forgiven our debtors. And lead us not into temptation, but deliver us from the evil one.'"

Knowing God more also means knowing how to talk to Him. Jesus, in His great kindness, gave us a model for prayer: The Lord's Prayer. It's not a script to recite mindlessly, but a guide to shape our conversations with the Father.

Prayer includes:

- Adoration: Honoring God's greatness and holiness.
- Submission: Yielding to His will and kingdom agenda.
- Petition: Asking for daily provision and spiritual sustenance.
- Confession: Seeking forgiveness and offering it to others.
- Protection: Requesting deliverance from temptation and evil.

Our prayers don't have to be long or complicated; they simply need to be sincere. Approach Him with honesty, trust, and a heart ready to hear from Him. The more we talk to God, the more we will come to know His heart—and the more we will experience His love, His power, and His presence in deeper and more personal ways.

Bold Transparency Leads to Greater Intimacy

Psalm 51:1-2 (NIV) — "Have mercy on me, O God, according to your unfailing love; according to your great compassion blot out my transgressions. Wash away all my iniquity and cleanse me from my sin."

Authenticity in prayer is not optional—it is critical. We pray to an all-knowing God. It is impossible to hide anything from Him, so why even try? True intimacy with the Father is birthed through bold transparency.

David's heartfelt prayer of repentance after his sin with Bathsheba demonstrates this beautifully. David didn't attempt to shift the blame onto Bathsheba or anyone else. He owned his failures completely and brought the full weight of his sin before the Lord. He acknowledged not only the specific incident but the frailty of his human nature. This is intimacy. Holding nothing back. Covering nothing. Trusting fully.

Intimacy is most powerfully developed when we lay everything bare before the Lord, knowing that His love remains steadfast.

I can recall a powerful season in my life when "Bold Transparency" changed everything. I was driving to Mayport, Florida, after preaching at Mt. Sinai Holy Church in Kinston, North Carolina. As I drove, I began pouring out my heart to God—everything

I was carrying internally, externally, about ministry, the military—everything. I didn't dress up my words. I simply spoke from my heart. Tears streamed down my face as I laid it all before Him. For hours, I prayed and cried out to God.

When I was finished, I had never felt closer to the Lord. It was as if the Father whispered, "I was waiting for you to do this." That moment of complete vulnerability broke chains I didn't even realize I was still carrying. No longer could the enemy hold guilt over me. If he tried, my response was simple: "I already told God about it."

Glory to God! It was liberating. It was healing. And it brought an intimacy with the Father that I had never known before.

Beloved, I invite you to try it. Bold Transparency. Your heavenly Father is not afraid of the material you release to Him in prayer. Jesus provides a safe space to divulge everything you can't tell anyone else. And when you do, you will find yourself drawn closer to the Father's heart in a way you never imagined.

The Tension with Request and Sovereignty

1 Samuel 1:10-11 (NIV) — "In her deep anguish Hannah prayed to the Lord, weeping bitterly. And she made a vow, saying, 'Lord Almighty, if you will only look on your servant's misery and remember me, and not forget your servant but give her a son, then I will give him to the Lord for all the days of his life.'"

2 Corinthians 12:7-9 (NIV) — "Therefore, in order to keep me from becoming conceited, I was given a thorn in my flesh, a messenger of Satan, to torment me. Three times I pleaded with the Lord to take it away from me. But He said to me, 'My grace is sufficient for you, for My power is made perfect in weakness.' Therefore I will boast all the more gladly about my weaknesses, so that Christ's power may rest on me."

Sometimes in prayer, we encounter the "tension" between our requests and God's sovereign will. This tension strengthens our relationship with Him and deepens our respect for His sovereignty.

In any close relationship, tension is inevitable. Even in marriage, friction can arise over differing opinions or desires. Yet, in healthy, mature relationships, one partner often defers to the other out of love, unity, and trust. In our relationship with Christ, the same is true—except on a much greater level.

Our love for God never overrides His sovereignty. He is supreme, and He knows what is best. His decisions are always just, always righteous, and always rooted in love.

In the military, subordinates are trained to defer to senior officers, trusting that their orders align with the standards of justice and duty. How much more should we, as believers, defer to the ultimate authority of God, who operates with perfect wisdom and love?

Hannah and Paul's experiences illustrate this tension vividly. Hannah prayed earnestly for a child and God said "yes," blessing her with Samuel, a prophet who would impact generations. Paul, on the other hand, pleaded for the removal of a "thorn" in his flesh, but God said "no," assuring him that His grace was sufficient.

Both faced real struggles—Hannah, the pain of barrenness and ridicule; Paul, the agony of persistent affliction. Yet God responded differently. The key is this: maturity is demonstrated when we "yield" to the Father, even when His answer isn't what we hoped for.

Yielding when you don't want to—that's where true spiritual growth happens. It refines our trust, deepens our intimacy, and sharpens our witness.

Beloved, we do not have to struggle. We simply yield. Lay down your right to want something different from what God desires to give. Trust His sovereignty. Trust His heart.

Growing in Dependency Further Tethers You to the Father's Heart

2 Chronicles 20:12 (NIV) — "Our God, will you not judge them? For we have no power to face this vast army that is attacking us. We do not know what to do, but our eyes are on you."

Prayer is essential at every stage of life and in every situation. A vital sign of growth and maturity in our prayer lives is learning to include God in everything. The more we engage God about every aspect of our lives, the more comfortable and natural our communication with Him becomes.

One of the most powerful aspects of prayer is the access we have to the Father. While many chase opportunities to speak with kings, queens, or celebrities, we—the believers—have the incredible privilege of speaking directly with the King of Kings and the Lord of Lords.

Jehoshaphat's story is profound. After leading a spiritual reformation in Judah, he was immediately confronted by a coalition of enemies intent on destruction. Instead of panicking or relying solely on military strength, Jehoshaphat turned to God first in private prayer.

Beloved, let me encourage you—do not let your prayer life only be about praying in public. It must be cultivated in private first. When we pray privately, sincerely seeking God's face, it empowers our public prayers with authenticity and spiritual authority.

Jehoshaphat's public prayer, particularly his confession, "Lord, we do not know what to do, but our eyes are on you," is a profound display of dependency. It showed Judah that even their king recognized the limitations of his own power and taught them that when facing hard times, God must be our first resort through prayer.

Jehoshaphat demonstrated that a heart anchored in private prayer naturally overflows into powerful public intercession. His deep dependence drew him closer to the Father's heart—and God responded in a mighty way. A prophetic word was released: *"The battle is not yours, but the Lord's."* That single declaration changed everything. From that moment, destruction came upon Judah's enemies—not through military strength, but through divine intervention. And it all began with Jehoshaphat's intimate, heartfelt prayer of intercession.

Grow in dependency. Pray in private. Seek His heart daily. And you will find yourself tethered more securely to the Father's heart than ever before.

Co-Laboring with God Through Intercession

1 Timothy 2:1-2 (NIV) — "I urge, then, first of all, that petitions, prayers, intercession, and thanksgiving be made for all people— for kings and all those in authority, that we may live peaceful and quiet lives in all godliness and holiness."

Throughout Scripture, the importance of prayer and intercession is repeatedly emphasized. Intercession, when done with a sincere heart, is not self-centered but outward-focused—lifting others, national concerns, and global needs before God.

Jesus' High Priestly Prayer in John 17 modeled the significance of leaders, ministers, and disciples engaging God in intercession. Jesus prayed for unity, protection, and sanctification for His disciples and for all who would believe through them.

Moses' prayers in Exodus 32 and Numbers 14 reveal a powerful dynamic: an intercessor pleading with God on behalf of a rebellious people, leading to divine mercy instead of judgment. Paul's letters to the churches are filled with intercessory prayers, asking for spiritual wisdom, growth, love, and strength for believers (Ephesians 1:15-23; 3:14-21; Philippians 1:9-11; Colossians 1:9-12; 2 Thessalonians 1:11-12).

Intercession is powerful because it interrupts the status quo. It calls upon heaven to intervene in human affairs—challenging systems of injustice, disrupting patterns of evil, and bringing hope to the hopeless.

True intercession stands in the gap for:

- Those who cannot or do not pray.
- Those who cause harm and need a heart transformation.
- National, state, and local leaders.
- Churches, pastors, and spiritual leaders.
- The hurting, the broken, the forgotten, and the marginalized.

Intercession is mobile, sacred, and transformational. It collaborates with God, invoking His power and authority on behalf of others. It is both a privilege and a responsibility to participate in God's redemptive work through prayer.

When we intercede, we join God in His mission. We labor with Him spiritually, mentally, economically, and socially. Intercession demands a heart that sees beyond self—one that carries the burdens of others with compassion and conviction.

We need more intercessors. We need more holy partnerships with God. The outcomes of faithful intercession are tangible: peace, quietness, godliness, and holiness in our nations, communities, and homes, just as 1 Timothy 2:1-2 declares.

Beloved, will you answer the call to stand in the gap?

Reflection Questions

1. How can you cultivate a more reverent and authentic posture when approaching God in prayer?

2. In what areas of your life are you struggling to yield to God's sovereignty, and how can you trust Him more deeply?

3. How is your private prayer life shaping and strengthening your public expressions of faith?

4. Who are the individuals, communities, or leaders that God is prompting you to regularly intercede for?

5. How can consistent, bold, and transparent communication with God tether your heart more securely to the Father's heart?

Application Activities

1. Create a Prayer Space: Set up a dedicated space in your home or workplace that encourages focused and uninterrupted time with God.

2. Practice Bold Transparency: Spend time in prayer this week being completely open with God—share your struggles, fears, joys, and dreams without filtering your words.

3. Yield in Prayer: Identify one personal desire and intentionally yield it to God's will, praying "Not my will, but Yours be done."

4. Intercede Intentionally: Choose three individuals or causes to lift in daily intercession for a full week, asking God for specific breakthroughs.

5. Record Your Journey: Start a prayer journal to capture your prayers, God's responses, and reflections on how your intimacy with Him is growing over time.

CHAPTER 10
Drawing Closer to God Through Fasting

Matthew 6:16-18 (NIV) — "When you fast, do not look somber as the hypocrites do, for they disfigure their faces to show others they are fasting... But when you fast, put oil on your head and wash your face, so that it will not be obvious to others that you are fasting, but only to your Father, who is unseen."

Jesus' Teaching on Fasting: Do It in Secret, Not for Show

The way we approach fasting matters deeply. Jesus Himself made it clear: there is a distinct difference between the sincere heart that fasts for God and the showy spirit that fasts for attention. God knows the difference. And if we pay attention to Jesus' guidelines, we will know the difference too.

Fasting is not a boastful act; it is a humble sacrifice aimed at reaping great spiritual rewards. It appeals to God, not to religious leaders, family, or friends. When fasting becomes a spectacle, the fleeting applause of people is all the reward there is — and it holds no eternal value.

The secret place with God is sacred. It is where spiritual transactions happen. It is in the secret place that prayers are answered, hearts are changed, and divine strategies are downloaded.

Our prayer should be: "Lord, help me to approach fasting with humility, sacrifice, and the understanding that this sacred act is between You and me."

Fasting: A Lifestyle, Not Just an Event

Anna's Life of Fasting and Prayer

> "And then as a widow until she was eighty-four. She never left the temple but worshiped night and day, fasting and praying."
>
> — Luke 2:37 (NIV)

True fasting is a way of life, not a one-time event.

Many treat fasting like a spiritual "fire alarm" — only breaking it out when emergencies arise. Others use it ceremonially, especially during seasons like Lent, as a gesture of temporary devotion. But beloved, I invite you to a higher perspective.

Fasting isn't about "getting God's attention" as if He were distant. It's about aligning ourselves with His heart, His mind, and His will. When we embrace fasting as a regular practice, we heighten our spiritual sensitivity and deepen our intimacy with Him.

Anna's life is a beautiful example. Day and night, she dedicated herself to worship, fasting, and prayer. Her devotion was not seasonal but steadfast. She wasn't chasing blessings; she was chasing God Himself. And God rewarded her devotion by allowing her to witness the Messiah.

Let's not treat fasting like a genie lamp. Let's make it a way of life — a continual posture of seeking God's presence. Tapping into the Mind of God and His Thoughts.

Daniel's Fast for Understanding and Revelation

> "At that time, I, Daniel, mourned for three weeks. I ate no choice food; no meat or wine touched my lips; and I used no lotions at all until the three weeks were over."
>
> — Daniel 10:2-3 (NIV)

Daniel fasted to seek divine insight. His desire wasn't material gain but spiritual revelation. Through fasting, Daniel tapped into the mind of God.

Other powerful examples include:

- Jehoshaphat's Fast for Deliverance — 2 Chronicles 20:3
- Israel's Fast for Victory — Judges 20:26
- Hannah's Fast for a Child — 1 Samuel 1:7-8

- David's Fast for His Child's Life — 2 Samuel 12:16
- Ezra's Fast for Protection and Guidance — Ezra 8:21-23
- Esther's Fast for Protection and Favor — Esther 4:16
- Fasting for Spiritual Breakthrough — Matthew 17:21; Isaiah 58:6

Each fast was an act of deep spiritual engagement — a desperate reach for God's hand and voice. They understood that fasting wasn't about manipulating God; it was about posturing themselves to receive His wisdom, favor, and intervention.

The "Who" of Fasting: Sacrificing for the Sake of Relationship

"Paul and Barnabas appointed elders for them in each church and, with prayer and fasting, committed them to the Lord."

— Acts 14:23 (NIV)

"After fasting forty days and forty nights, he was hungry."

— Matthew 4:2 (NIV)

Every believer must find opportunities to engage in this sacred practice. Even Jesus fasted. After forty days and nights, Satan tempted Him, first appealing to His physical hunger: "Turn these stones into bread." But Jesus' response reveals kingdom living: "Man shall not live on bread alone, but on every word that comes from the mouth of God" (Matthew 4:4).

Fasting prepared Jesus for spiritual warfare. It sharpened His discernment, strengthened His resolve, and fortified His soul against the enemy's twisted attempts to manipulate Scripture.

Through fasting, Jesus demonstrated that reliance on God supersedes reliance on physical needs. Fasting reminds us that our sustenance, hope, and strength are found in God alone.

If fasting was necessary for Jesus, how much more is it necessary for us?

When you fast, reflect on what outcomes you are seeking. Victory? Clarity? Strength? Revelation? Draw near to God, and He will draw near to you.

If the servant is not greater than the Master, fasting must become part of our spiritual journey too — equipping us to stand firm against the enemy of our souls.

Fasting fuels our spirit, renews our mind, and brings our flesh under submission. It teaches us dependency on God and increases our sensitivity to the Holy Spirit.

Scripture for Meditation

"Is not this the kind of fasting I have chosen: to loose the chains of injustice and untie the cords of the yoke, to set the oppressed free and break every yoke?"
— Isaiah 58:6 (NIV)

How to Fast?

There are a variety of ways believers approach fasting within the body of Christ. Traditionally, fasting has focused on abstaining from food. For those with medical conditions, it's important to exercise wisdom and adjust accordingly. A no-food fast can be done for designated hours of the day or extended over a 24-hour period with only water. Others may choose a juice fast—consuming only natural fruit juices while refraining from solid food.

Some opt for a Daniel-style fast, which includes eating only vegetables, fruits, nuts, and legumes over a set period, such as 21 days. Still others fast by abstaining from things that have become deeply consuming—such as television, social media, sweets, or other habits.

At its core, fasting is about breaking dependency on distractions or desires that compete for our devotion. It is a sacred practice of setting oneself apart—body, mind, and spirit—to draw closer to God in surrender and spiritual clarity.

In addition, the time set aside for fasting should be filled with other spiritual practices—such as prayer, worship, Scripture study, and meditation. Without these components, fasting loses its spiritual purpose and becomes little more than a diet. True fasting is not just about what you give up, but how you press in to connect more deeply with God.

Reflections

1. What is my true motivation for fasting? Is it to be seen by others or to grow closer to God?

2. How can I make fasting a regular part of my spiritual life rather than an emergency tool?

3. In what areas of my life do I need divine revelation or breakthrough?

4. Have I ever experienced greater spiritual clarity or strength after fasting? What was that like?

5. How can fasting help me align my thoughts more closely with the mind of Christ?

Application Exercises

1. Plan a personal fast: Choose a day this month to fast and spend focused time in prayer and Scripture.

2. Read Daniel 10: Journal what God reveals to you about seeking Him through fasting.

3. Pray for a fasting lifestyle: Ask God to help you adopt fasting not just as an event, but as part of your worship.

4. Identify a breakthrough area: Fast specifically for clarity, victory, or healing in one area of your life.

5. Fast with community: Partner with a friend or small group for a day of fasting, sharing prayer points and encouragement.

CHAPTER 11

Connecting with God in Worship

The Why of Worship

There is something powerful about worshipping God. Worship is ascribing to God who He is to us, both personally and based on how He has revealed Himself through Scripture. It is personal to God. In the Decalogue, God instructed the children of Israel not to worship any engraved images or idols, emphasizing that no other gods should come before Him. Worship is sacred to God; it is a spiritual act that He reserves exclusively for Himself.

Worship can be expressed in many beautiful ways: through music, dance, speech, gestures, instruments, and even through the faithful performance of our work and talents. In every expression, worship points back to detailing who God is.

I am a worshipper because Scripture declares that we were created to worship. One of our divine responsibilities is to tell God who He is to us. Some call Him Mighty God, Counselor, Marvelous, Lover of My Soul, Way Maker, The Light, Prince of Peace — and the list goes on into infinity because God is just that wonderful. Our expression of worship is limitless!

Worship is unique because it is one thing God does not do for Himself; He relies on His creation to worship Him. In heaven, worship is continual. Worship was so important that when Satan sought to steal it for himself, he was cast out of heaven along with every angel who joined him. God does not play about worship.

Therefore, we must be vigilant that nothing and no one else becomes the object of our worship. Our anthem must be: "To You alone is my worship!"

According to John 4:24, "God is spirit, and his worshipers must worship in the Spirit and in truth." This powerful truth reminds us that God is actively seeking true worshipers. It emphasizes that God is not just interested in the act of worship but deeply concerned with the heart of the worshiper. He examines who is worshipping, why they are worshipping, and who or what they are worshipping.

Worship is not a performance; it is a matter of the heart. Let's get our worship right because getting it wrong is too costly. Worship misdirected led to Satan's downfall and the fall of humanity in the garden. Worship rightly placed leads to intimacy with God, divine favor, and eternal reward.

Our worship should be pure, sincere, and aligned with God's truth. Every day, we must make the choice to worship God for who He is, not merely for what He does. True worship transforms us and draws us deeper into the heart of God.

My Personal Experience with Worship unto the Lord

Worship has always been a safe space for me—a sacred realm where I meet with God and He meets with me.

It has been my practice to close my eyes, lift my hands, and begin to utter words of adoration about who God is to me.

I often find myself saying: "Lord, I love You. Lord, I appreciate You. You are kind, You are love, You are life, You are my everything."

Oftentimes, I run out of descriptions and find myself repeating words over and over again, because God is that—and so much more.

The lifting of my hands is my way of surrendering Kevin—all that I am and all that is within me. Everything is captured and lifted unto the Lord as a sacrifice of self so that God has full view of all of me.

I surrender the good, the bad, the indifferent, and the progressing. All of me is lifted up to the Lord as a spiritual sacrifice.

Although I do not have a singer's voice, I often sing songs of the church that proclaim the majesty and wonder of God. I love to worship the Lord by singing hymns like *The Solid Rock* or Pastor Andraé Crouch's *My Tribute*. Another hymn that lifts me is *Holy, Holy, Holy*—songs that ascribe glory to God and declare who He is to me.

It is often in worship that I experience the manifest presence of God. It is as if He comes and dwells in that sacred space—gathering up all the worship I lift to Him—and He dances in it, sings in it, sits in it, and enjoys it.

That's how I imagine God receiving my worship.

"Here's my worship. All of my worship."

That's the attitude and mindset I carry—not just during a public worship service but even within the walls of my own home.

Though I am not a professional keyboard player, I am self-taught and often find myself jumping on the keyboard to make melodies unto the Lord. Hours can pass by in what feels like only moments.

There is such a sense of fulfillment just talking about and to the Lord through music. Worship, for me, has been—and continues to be—a safe and sacred place to commune with God.

Even when I listen to instrumental worship music, it ministers to my heart. I find my eyes closed, my mind focused on the awesomeness of the Lord.

That's worship for me.

I also have a deep appreciation for congregational worship—the gathering of the saints to sing songs, to give together, to hear the reading of the Word, and to receive the preaching of the Word.

All of it is worship to me. Joining with other believers to talk about the Lord of Lords gives me a spiritual high.

As a Pentecostal, worship often lifts me into a place of spiritual ecstasy—where I dance before the Lord, sing with uninhibited joy, and at times, lay prostrate in complete surrender to His presence.

It is in worship that I have experienced healing—of the soul, spirit, and body.

It is in worship that I have heard the voice of the Lord giving clarity, direction, and prophetic utterances.

It is in worship that I have experienced the refilling of the Holy Ghost, preparing me for the next level of service unto the Lord.

Worship has been a place of restoration and renewal in my life and in my walk with Christ. That is why I do not arrive late to worship. I don't leave worship early either, because God can show up in manifestation at any moment during those precious times.

I must also say that I am a lover of liturgical worship. I love to hear the anthems, to participate in the responsive readings, and to join the faithful in ascribing the greatness of the Lord in the sanctuary.

I see the sacred gathering of the saints—the movement of the liturgy, the dashing of the smokes and incense, the vibrant coloration of clergy garb, and the sacred furniture of the Lord's house. All of it is worship for me.

I even find worship experiences in the context of nature. To hear creation make the sounds of a thousand musicals and sonnets through the birds and other animals is sacred and spiritually filling. Oftentimes, I kayak on calm waters and gather a deep sense of God's presence with me.

As the waters clash and sing praises to our God, I feel Him there. The floating turtles, the dipping sea gulls, the smooth gliding dolphins—all assemble a natural sanctuary where worship exudes from the very fabric of creation itself.

Dear reader, never limit your concept of worship experiences.

Never limit where it can happen.

How it can happen.

When it can happen.

If God is present, and He is glorified—it is worship.

Let's Look Deeper into Scripture to Gain Greater Clarity About Worship

Worship Because God is Worthy

"You are worthy, our Lord and God, to receive glory and honor and power, for You created all things, and by Your will they were created and have their being."
— Revelation 4:11

"For great is the Lord and most worthy of praise; He is to be feared above all gods."
— Psalm 96:4

Worship Because of His Holiness

"Ascribe to the Lord the glory due His name; bring an offering and come before Him. Worship the Lord in the splendor of His holiness."
— 1 Chronicles 16:29

"And they were calling to one another: 'Holy, holy, holy is the Lord Almighty; the whole earth is full of His glory.'"
— Isaiah 6:3

Worship Because We Were Created to Worship

"Yet a time is coming and has now come when the true worshipers will worship the Father in the Spirit and in truth, for they are the kind of worshipers the Father seeks. God is spirit, and His worshipers must worship in the Spirit and in truth."
— John 4:24-25

"Let everything that has breath praise the Lord. Praise the Lord!"
— Psalm 150:6

Worship Because of His Great Love and Mercy

"Because of the Lord's great love we are not consumed, for His compassions never fail. They are new every morning; great is Your faithfulness."
— Lamentations 3:22-23

"Therefore, I urge you, brothers and sisters, in view of God's mercy, to offer your bodies as a living sacrifice, holy and pleasing to God—this is your true and proper worship."
— Romans 12:1

Worship Because of His Power and Majesty

"Come, let us bow down in worship, let us kneel before the Lord our Maker; for He is our God and we are the people of His pasture, the flock under His care."
— Psalm 95:6-7

"Great is the Lord and most worthy of praise; His greatness no one can fathom."
— Psalm 145:3

Worship Because He is the Only True God

"He is the one you praise; He is your God, who performed for you those great and awesome wonders you saw with your own eyes."
— Deuteronomy 10:21

"Jesus said to him, 'Away from me, Satan! For it is written: Worship the Lord your God, and serve Him only.'"

— Matthew 4:10

Worship Because of His Salvation

"Praise the Lord, my soul; all my inmost being, praise His holy name. Praise the Lord, my soul, and forget not all His benefits."

— Psalm 103:1-2

"Therefore God exalted Him to the highest place and gave Him the name that is above every name, that at the name of Jesus every knee should bow, in heaven and on earth and under the earth, and every tongue acknowledge that Jesus Christ is Lord, to the glory of God the Father."

— Philippians 2:9-11

The How of Worship

Worship is not limited to a posture or a song. It is a lifestyle that acknowledges God with every fiber of our being. David Dances Before the Lord: 2 Samuel 6:14 — "Wearing a linen ephod, David was dancing before the Lord with all his might."

Nehemiah and the Israelites Raised Their Hands: Nehemiah 8:6 — "Ezra praised the Lord, the great God; and all the people lifted their hands and responded, 'Amen! Amen!' Then they bowed down and worshiped the Lord with their faces to the ground."

Paul and Silas sung in prison: Acts 16:25 — "About midnight Paul and Silas were praying and singing hymns to God, and the other prisoners were listening to them."

Abraham Sacrificed in Worship: Genesis 22:5 — "He said to his servants, 'Stay here with the donkey while I and the boy go over there. We will worship and then we will come back to you.'"

Mary Anointed Jesus' Feet: John 12:3 — "Then Mary took about a pint of pure nard, an expensive perfume; she poured it on Jesus' feet and wiped His feet with her hair. And the house was filled with the fragrance of the perfume."

Ezra Led Worship and Repentance: Ezra 10:1 — "While Ezra was praying and confessing, weeping and throwing himself down before the house of God, a large crowd of Israelites—men, women and children—gathered around him. They too wept bitterly."

The When of Worship

Worship is not confined to a service or a specific day. We worship in every season of life, in every circumstance.

Job Worshiped in Suffering: Job 1:20-21 — "At this, Job got up and tore his robe and shaved his head. Then he fell to the ground in worship and said: 'Naked I came from my mother's womb, and naked I will depart. The Lord gave and the Lord has taken away; may the name of the Lord be praised.'"

Moses Worshiped After Encountering God: Exodus 34:8 — "Moses bowed to the ground at once and worshiped."

Hannah Worshiped After Answered Prayer: 1 Samuel 1:27-28 — "I prayed for this child, and the Lord has granted me what I asked of him. So now I give him to the Lord. For his whole life he will be given over to the Lord." And he worshiped the Lord there.

A final thought on worship: true worship is God-centered. It focuses solely on who God is—His nature, His glory, His holiness. Anything else falls short of being worship in spirit and in truth. Worship is the communion of the believer's spirit with the heart of God. It's not defined by tempo or style—it's not simply a slow song—but rather by content: a song, a sound, or a posture that attempts to express the greatness of God, even within the limits of human language. If you truly desire to draw closer to Him, lean into worship. That's where intimacy begins.

Father, thank You for meeting us in the sacred spaces we call worship. Whether in the sanctuary or on the sea, whether through music or through stillness, may our hearts always rise to You in spirit and in truth. Teach us to worship You with all that we are. Receive our offering. In Jesus' name, Amen.

Reflection Questions

1. Why do you believe worship is so important to God?

2. What forms of worship resonate most deeply with your spirit?

3. How does worship impact your relationship with Jesus?

4. In what ways can you guard your worship from becoming distracted or misplaced?

5. What does it mean to you to worship "in spirit and in truth"?

Application Exercises

1. Daily Worship Journal: For one week, write down a daily reflection of how you worshipped God that day.

2. Create a Worship Playlist: Compile songs that lift your spirit and draw your heart closer to God.

3. Offer a Talent to God: Choose one of your talents (art, writing, service, teaching) and intentionally use it to glorify God this week.

4. Sacrifice of Time: Dedicate an hour this week to uninterrupted worship and prayer, free from distractions.

5. Worship Walk: Take a walk and worship God aloud for who He is and what He has done in your life.

CHAPTER 12

Meditating on the Word for Deeper Intimacy

Words matter. Words have power.

In everyday life, people are drawn to words that affirm them. When someone takes the time to express appreciation, encouragement, or recognition, it reflects understanding, value, and connection. Words convey meaning. When you hear someone say, "I love you," it signals that they see the treasure of who you are and affirm it with emotion and sincerity.

Scripture underscores the power of words: Proverbs 18:21 (NKJV) — "Death and life are in the power of the tongue."

Words can tear down or build up. They can inspire, clear confusion, bring enlightenment, and expand our intellectual and emotional capacity. Words are indeed powerful.

Understanding the power of words helps us grasp why the Word of God is so vital to our lives. His Word carries unparalleled impact for anyone willing to let it take root. It brings clarity, meaning, correction, strength—everything we need.

As Paul reminds us: 2 Timothy 3:16-17 (NIV) — "All Scripture is God-breathed and is useful for teaching, rebuking, correcting and training in righteousness, so that the servant of God may be thoroughly equipped for every good work."

We cannot function effectively in the Kingdom or navigate this world without a deep connection to the Word of God.

Think about it this way: when you read a person's biography, you gain insight into their dreams, values, and experiences. Their story connects with parts of your own journey. In the same way, the Bible is the biography of the Lord. It reveals His character, His likes and dislikes, His Kingdom standards, and the principles for living.

The Word of God is life-giving, teaching us the "language of the Father" to discern what He has said, what He is saying, and what He may say about our lives.

"Your word is a lamp to my feet and a light to my path."

— Psalm 119:105 (NKJV)

Without His Word, we would be lost. But with it, we have a divine roadmap from earth to heaven. If you want to know Him more—read His bio.

Let's peruse the Lord's BIO for the purpose of meditation.

The Approach to Meditation on the Word

When I suggest the practice of meditation, I am inviting you to:
- Select a text that focuses on an immediate topic for you.
- Pray and ask the Lord to open your understanding.
- Read the text two times.
- Read the broader chapter where the text is located.
- Read the text a third time and write down your thoughts.
- Study any parts of the text with a commentary, Bible dictionary, lexicon, or concordance.
- Determine how the text can be applied in your life.

Meditation on the Word: Key Scriptures

Meditation Leads to Success and Prosperity

"Keep this Book of the Law always on your lips; meditate on it day and night, so that you may be careful to do everything written in it. Then you will be prosperous and successful."

— Joshua 1:8

The Righteous Delight in Meditating on God's Word

"But his delight is in the law of the Lord, and on his law he meditates day and night. That person is like a tree planted by streams of water, which yields its fruit in season and whose leaf does not wither—whatever they do prospers."

— Psalm 1:2-3

Meditation on the Word Brings Closeness to God

"On my bed I remember You; I think of You through the watches of the night. Because You are my help, I sing in the shadow of Your wings."

— Psalm 63:6-7

Meditating on God's Deeds Strengthens Faith

"I will consider all Your works and meditate on all Your mighty deeds."

— Psalm 77:12

Meditation Fills the Heart with God's Wisdom

"I meditate on Your precepts and consider Your ways."

— Psalm 119:15

Meditating on God's Word Brings Understanding

"I have more insight than all my teachers, for I meditate on Your statutes."

— Psalm 119:99

God's Word is a Lamp Through Meditation

"Your word is a lamp for my feet, a light on my path."

— Psalm 119:105

Meditation Leads to an Unshakable Faith

"You will keep in perfect peace those whose minds are steadfast, because they trust in You."

— Isaiah 26:3

The Mind That Stays on God is Blessed

"'For My thoughts are not your thoughts, neither are your ways My ways,' declares the Lord. 'As the heavens are higher than the earth, so are My ways higher than your ways and My thoughts than your thoughts.'"

— Isaiah 55:8-9

Jesus Taught the Importance of Abiding in His Word

"If you remain in Me and My words remain in you, ask whatever you wish, and it will be done for you."

— John 15:7

Meditation Transforms the Mind

"Do not conform to the pattern of this world, but be transformed by the renewing of your mind. Then you will be able to test and approve what God's will is—His good, pleasing and perfect will."

— Romans 12:2

Thinking on What is Noble and Pure Brings Us Closer to God

"Finally, brothers and sisters, whatever is true, whatever is noble, whatever is right, whatever is pure, whatever is lovely, whatever is admirable—if anything is excellent or praiseworthy—think about such things."

— Philippians 4:8

Meditating on Christ Deepens Our Understanding

"Let the message of Christ dwell among you richly as you teach and admonish one another with all wisdom through psalms, hymns, and songs from the Spirit, singing to God with gratitude in your hearts."

— Colossians 3:16

Meditation Helps Us Set Our Minds on Heavenly Things

"Set your minds on things above, not on earthly things."

— Colossians 3:2

The Word of God is Alive and Works in Our Hearts

"For the word of God is alive and active. Sharper than any double-edged sword, it penetrates even to dividing soul and spirit, joints and marrow; it judges the thoughts and attitudes of the heart."

— Hebrews 4:12

Why Meditate on the Word?

The Word of God is Living and Powerful

"For the word of God is alive and active. Sharper than any double-edged sword, it penetrates even to dividing soul and spirit, joints and marrow; it judges the thoughts and attitudes of the heart."

— Hebrews 4:12

The Word is Inspired by God

"All Scripture is God-breathed and is useful for teaching, rebuking, correcting and training in righteousness, so that the servant of God may be thoroughly equipped for every good work."

— 2 Timothy 3:16-17

The Word Gives Wisdom and Guidance

"Your word is a lamp for my feet, a light on my path."

— Psalm 119:105

The Word of God is Eternal

"The grass withers and the flowers fall, but the word of our God endures forever."

— Isaiah 40:8

The Word Cleanses and Sanctifies

"To make her holy, cleansing her by the washing with water through the word."

— Ephesians 5:26

The Word Produces Faith

"Consequently, faith comes from hearing the message, and the message is heard through the word about Christ."

— Romans 10:17

The Word of God is Truth

"Sanctify them by the truth; your word is truth."

— John 17:17

The Word Brings Blessings When Obeyed

"Do not merely listen to the word, and so deceive yourselves. Do what it says."

— James 1:22

The Word is a Weapon Against the Enemy

"Take the helmet of salvation and the sword of the Spirit, which is the word of God."

— Ephesians 6:17

The Word of God Gives Understanding

"The unfolding of your words gives light; it gives understanding to the simple."

— Psalm 119:130

The Word Keeps Us from Sin

"I have hidden your word in my heart that I might not sin against you."

— Psalm 119:11

The Word Stands Forever

"Heaven and earth will pass away, but my words will never pass away."

— Matthew 24:35

The Word Nourishes Our Spirit

"Jesus answered, 'It is written: Man shall not live on bread alone, but on every word that comes from the mouth of God.'"

— Matthew 4:4

The Word Brings Freedom

"To the Jews who had believed him, Jesus said, 'If you hold to my teaching, you are really my disciples. Then you will know the truth, and the truth will set you free.'"

— John 8:31-32

The Word of God Accomplishes His Purpose

"So is my word that goes out from my mouth: It will not return to me empty but will accomplish what I desire and achieve the purpose for which I sent it."

— Isaiah 55:11

Key Takeaway

The more we meditate on God's Word, the more we begin to think, speak, and live like Christ. His Word becomes the lens through which we see the world, the anchor that steadies our soul, and the fuel that propels us into our divine purpose. Let the Bible Speak.

Beloved, I pray you have heard the many messages that have gone forth—each one designed to stir your spirit and draw you closer to the heart of Christ. Every word, every passage, every prompting was meant to invite you into deeper relationship with Him and to awaken a greater sensitivity to His voice.

Why is this so important? Because when you know His Word, you begin to recognize His voice. You start to understand not only what He has said, but what He is saying even now—and what He may yet say concerning the circumstances of your life. His Word becomes the lens through which you see the world and the anchor by which you stand.

As you take time to meditate on Scripture, day by day, your walk with Jesus will grow stronger. His thoughts will shape your thoughts. His heart will mold your heart. Before you know it, you'll find yourself talking like Him, thinking like Him, and living like Him—all because you allowed His Word to dwell richly within you. "Let the word of Christ dwell in you richly..."—Colossians 3:16 (NIV)

Let the Bible speak to you.

Let it change you.

Let it lead you into life more abundant.

Closing Prayer

Father, thank You for the precious gift of Your Word. Thank You for inviting me into deeper fellowship with You through Scripture.

As I meditate on Your truth, open my heart and mind to receive fresh revelation. Let Your Word shape my thoughts, guard my heart, and guide my steps.

Teach me to love what You love, to value what You value, and to walk in obedience to Your voice.

Plant Your Word deep within me, and cause it to bear fruit in every area of my life.

May my meditation on Your Word draw me closer to You, transform me into the likeness of Christ, and empower me to live out Your will on the earth.

I desire to know You more—through every verse, every principle, and every promise.

In Jesus' name, Amen.

Let's Know Him More—By Reading More About Him

Reflection Questions

1. What is one area of your life where you need the guidance of God's Word right now?

2. How does viewing the Bible as God's "biography" change your approach to reading it?

3. Which Scripture passage stood out to you most during your reading?

4. In what ways has meditating on God's Word brought you peace or clarity in the past?

5. What distractions often prevent you from meditating deeply on the Word, and how can you overcome them?

Application Exercises

1. Choose one passage from this chapter and spend a full week meditating on it daily.

2. Write a personal prayer based on a Scripture that spoke to your heart.

3. Memorize one verse from this chapter and recite it throughout your day.

4. Keep a meditation journal: each day, write a short reflection on how the Word is speaking to your current life circumstances.

5. Share a Scripture from your meditation time with a friend or family member to encourage them in their walk with Christ.

CHAPTER 13

Knowing Him More by Making Him Known

F aith was never designed to be hidden. True faith—the kind that grows, matures, and transforms—is meant to be shared. When we share what God has done in our lives, when we live out His love in the world, something incredible happens: our own relationship with Him deepens. Sharing Him doesn't dilute our faith; it multiplies it.

Many believers shy away from sharing their faith, thinking they need a degree in theology or a dramatic testimony. But God calls us to be witnesses, not experts. Every act of service, every word of encouragement, every demonstration of love is a testimony that points others to Him. And as we make Him known, we come to know Him more intimately ourselves.

The Biblical Mandate to Make God Known

When you experience something or someone that changes your life, your instinct is to tell others. The more you talk about them, the deeper their imprint becomes on your heart.

When I first met my wife, I couldn't stop sharing about her with family and friends. The more I spoke of her, the more I discovered about her, and the closer we became. I find it the same with God. The more I reflect on what He has done—in my life, through my life, and for my life—the more I am compelled to share Him with others.

This is the spirit behind Jesus' Great Commission in **Matthew 28:19-20**: "Therefore, go and make disciples of all nations, baptizing them in the name of the Father and of the Son and of the Holy Spirit, and teaching them to obey everything I have commanded you. And surely I am with you always, to the very end of the age."

Jesus charged His disciples not just to hold onto the truth, but to spread it. Teaching, baptizing, and sharing the kingdom principles they learned—this was their mission. As they spoke about the Kingdom, they grew stronger in their understanding of it.

When Jesus asked His disciples in **Matthew 16:15-17**, "But what about you?... Who do you say I am?" Peter answered, "You are the Messiah, the Son of the living God."

Jesus affirmed Peter's revelation and then revealed to Peter his identity in the Kingdom: "And I tell you that you are Peter, and on this rock I will build my church, and the gates of Hades will not overcome it."

Knowing Christ more led Peter to know himself more. Being a disciple of Jesus Christ isn't a passive title; it demands action. Just as ambassadors represent their countries, we represent the Kingdom of God. **2 Corinthians 5:20** reminds us: "We are therefore Christ's ambassadors, as though God were making his appeal through us. We implore you on Christ's behalf: Be reconciled to God."

Wherever you are—home, work, community—you are an ambassador of Christ. Through speech, service, work ethic, and advocacy, you make Him known.

Faith in Action: Living as a Testimony

Jesus intended for His followers to be active, not passive.

As a chaplain, I understand deeply that my interactions often shape how others perceive Christ. Even without quoting Scripture, the wisdom and counsel I offer are rooted in biblical truths.

No matter where you work—schools, hospitals, corporations—your integrity, kindness, empathy, and excellence testify to your faith. As **Galatians 5:22-23** says: "But the fruit of the Spirit is love, joy, peace, forbearance, kindness, goodness, faithfulness, gentleness and self-control. Against such things there is no law."

Our daily actions are living epistles, as Paul wrote in **2 Corinthians 3:2-3**: "You yourselves are our letter, written on our hearts, known and read by everyone. You show that you are a letter from Christ, the result of our ministry, written not with ink but with the Spirit of the living God."

When opportunities arise to share your story or your faith, trust that God has prepared those moments. People may forget our exact words, but they will remember how we made them feel—valued, loved, and seen

Overcoming Fear and Feelings of Inadequacy

You might be thinking, *"But it's not that easy!"* And you're right—fear and feelings of inadequacy often try to silence us. But here's the truth: **God doesn't call the qualified; He qualifies the called.**

Even Moses doubted himself because of his speech limitations, but God reassured him in Exodus 4:11–12: *"The Lord said to him, 'Who gave human beings their mouths?... Now go; I will help you speak and will teach you what to say.'"*

Today, we have even more opportunities to share our faith—through social media, blogs, videos, and other platforms that can carry the Gospel far beyond face-to-face conversations.

Above all, rely on the Holy Spirit. Jesus promised in John 14:26: *"But the Advocate, the Holy Spirit, whom the Father will send in my name, will teach you all things and will remind you of everything I have said to you."*

You don't have to be a Bible scholar to witness. Remember, Jesus chose ordinary fishermen—not religious elites—to be His first witnesses. Speak from your heart. Share what you know. Keep it simple and sincere. As Matthew 18:3 says: *"Truly I tell you, unless you change and become like little children, you will never enter the kingdom of heaven."* Childlike faith—honest and pure—often carries more weight than the most eloquent sermon.

And don't forget: you are not responsible for someone's salvation. That's God's role. As Paul said in 1 Corinthians 3:6: *"I planted the seed, Apollos watered it, but God has been making it grow."* Your role is to plant the seed—through your words, your actions, and the way you live.

Take time to prepare. Join a discipleship class. Read books and resources on evangelism. Most importantly, practice relational evangelism—build genuine connections, share your story, and offer prayer when the door opens.

You don't need to be perfect to be powerful. Just be available.

Here's a sample engagement with a nonbeliever that I had the opportunity to witness to:

Kevin: Hey, how you feeling today, brother?

Dwayne: Hey, I'm doing okay, man. I see y'all out here talking to people, huh?

Kevin: Yep! I'm glad I get the chance to talk with you today. Mind if I share something with you real quick?

Dwayne: Ah, yeah okay. I don't have a lot of time though, bro.

Kevin: No worries—I appreciate whatever time you can give. Do you go to church anywhere?

Dwayne: I used to, but I kinda strayed away. Too much drama in those churches, man. I just don't have time for all that.

Kevin: I get that. Can I ask—what do you know about Jesus Christ?

Dwayne: Oh yeah, I know He died and everything for all of us. He's God's Son.

Kevin: Man, that's right. And even more than that—He died for *you.*

Dwayne: Facts.

Kevin: I'm glad you know about Jesus. But do you have a personal relationship with Him?

Dwayne: What do you mean by that?

Kevin: Like—have you asked Him to be your Savior? Made Him Lord over your life?

Dwayne: Nah, I can't say I have.

Kevin: Mind if I show you how to do that?

Dwayne: Sure, I'm listening.

Kevin: It's simple. You just ask Jesus through prayer to forgive you of all your sins and commit to following Him from now on—that's called repentance. Then you believe that He is the Son of God, that He died on the cross for your sins, and that God raised Him from the dead on the third day. Do you believe that?

Dwayne: I'm willing to repent like you said. And yeah, I've heard about Jesus being God's Son, dying for us, and coming back on that Sunday morning, right?

Kevin: Yes sir!

Dwayne: I believe it.

Kevin: Well, Brother Dwayne, if you believe that, then all that's left is for us to pray and ask Christ to be your Savior.

Dwayne: I'm down, bro.

Kevin: Great. Mind if I place my hand on your shoulder while we pray—just as a sign of connection?

Dwayne: Sure, no problem.

Kevin: Repeat after me, brother Dwayne:

Kevin: Lord, forgive me of all my sins.

Dwayne: Lord, forgive me of all my sins.

Kevin: Father, I believe that Jesus is Your Son.

Dwayne: Father, I believe that Jesus is Your Son.

Kevin: I believe Jesus died on the cross for all my sins.

Dwayne: I believe Jesus died on the cross for all my sins.

Kevin: I believe You raised Him from the grave on the third day.

Dwayne: I believe You raised Him from the grave on the third day.

Kevin: And by confessing that, I am saved and in relationship with Jesus—starting right now.

Dwayne: And by confessing that, I am saved and in relationship with Jesus—starting right now.

Kevin: In Jesus' Name, Amen.

Dwayne: In Jesus' Name, Amen.

Kevin: Welcome to the family of God, my brother. Here's something to remind you of what happened today—and it's got my contact info on it too. I'd love to invite you to church with me this week. Is that cool?

Dwayne: Thank you, man. I feel good. I feel cleansed, bro. I'mma keep this with me. Yeah, man—hit me up. I'll come with you to church. I'm gonna give it a try.

Kevin: That's awesome, bro. Let's stay in touch. I'll see you Sunday.

Let me tell you—there's a deep joy that comes from sharing Christ with someone else. It strengthens your intimacy with Him in a powerful way. When something this good changes your life, you just can't keep it to yourself. Sharing your faith is your way of saying, *"I'm with Him—I'm with Jesus, and I'm not ashamed."* It's a bold declaration to the world and to anyone who will listen. If I truly love Him, I can't help but talk about Him to everyone I know.

The Holy Spirit is your guide, your comforter, and your helper in every conversation. This is what it means to truly know Him and make Him known—**a life of real intimacy.**

Reflection Questions

1. What fears or insecurities have held you back from sharing your faith?

2. How has your understanding of yourself deepened when you share about Christ?

3. In what areas of your life do you sense God calling you to be a greater ambassador for His Kingdom?

4. How has someone's act of faith influenced your spiritual journey?

5. What are some simple ways you can begin to make Christ known in your daily life?

Application Activities

1. Write a brief personal testimony that you can easily share in everyday conversations.

2. Pray and ask the Holy Spirit to guide you to one person this week to share your faith journey with.

3. Post an encouraging Scripture or testimony on your social media platform.

4. Identify a new setting (workplace, neighborhood, online community) where you can actively live out and share your faith.

5. Memorize Matthew 28:19-20 and 2 Corinthians 5:20 to strengthen your commitment as Christ's ambassador.

Final Reflection from the Author

As I bring this journey to a close, my heart is filled with gratitude—gratitude for the faithfulness of God and for the quiet work He does in every heart that dares to seek Him more.

Knowing Him More: A Journey from Belief to Greater Intimacy was never meant to be a mere book of lessons; it was always intended to be an invitation—a personal call to draw closer, to go deeper, and to experience the richness of relationship with the One who loved us first.

My prayer is that through these pages, your hunger for Christ has been stirred and your faith has been strengthened. I hope you have seen that intimacy with God is not reserved for a select few, but is available to every believer who chooses the path of faithful pursuit. Knowing Him more is not a destination to be reached, but a daily journey of trust, surrender, and discovery.

There will always be more to learn, more to experience, and more to receive from His hand. Yet the beauty of this pursuit is that God Himself is the reward. Not merely the blessings He gives, but His very presence is our greatest treasure.

As you continue forward, may you walk with greater confidence, listen with greater sensitivity, and love with greater devotion. May your life become a living testimony of what it looks like to truly know Him—and to make Him known.

Thank you for allowing me to walk alongside you in this sacred journey. May the pursuit never end. May the love never grow cold. And may you find, with every passing day, that He is more than enough. I hope you know him more than you did before and continue this journey of intimate discovery.

About The Author

Rev. Dr. Kevin m. Jackson is a passionate teacher, spiritual leader, and mentor whose life's mission is to help others deepen their relationship with Jesus Christ. as the founder and teacher of Ministry Moments, Dr. Jackson has devoted his ministry to equipping believers to live out their faith with purpose, intimacy, and unwavering devotion.

With a pastoral heart and a scholar's mind, Dr. Jackson bridges theological depth with everyday faith, making the profound truths of Scripture accessible and transformational for all believers. His journey has been marked by a relentless pursuit of Christ—not just knowing about Him, but knowing Him more deeply, more personally, and more intimately.

Through his preaching, teaching, and writing, Dr. Jackson invites readers to move beyond surface-level religion and into a faithful, vibrant relationship with the Living God. Knowing Him More: A Journey from Belief to Greater Intimacy reflects the heart of his ministry: to encourage, inspire, and challenge believers to seek Christ passionately and to live out their calling with boldness and love.

When he is not preaching, teaching, or writing, Dr. Jackson enjoys investing in the next generation of leaders, building up marriages, and serving alongside his beloved wife, Dr. Nila Nash-Jackson.

His greatest joy is seeing lives transformed by the power of God's Word—and helping others discover the abundant life that flows from knowing Him more.

Bibliography

Blackaby, Henry T. "Hearing God's Voice." Nashville: Broadman & Holman Publishers, 2002.

Quinn, Robert E. "Deep Change: Discovering the Leader Within." San Francisco: Jossey-Bass Publishers, 1996.

The Holy Bible, New International Version. Grand Rapids: Zondervan, 2011.

Ware, Frederick L. "African American Theology: An Introduction." Louisville: Westminster John Knox Press, 2008.

Made in the USA
Columbia, SC
04 July 2025

60337239R00063